Praise for Daniel Tobin's *Dusk, Empire*

Daniel Tobin's *Dusk, Empire* constitutes a potent distillation of a majestic career, wrought over many decades, that gives ample evidence of his position as one of the most accomplished and esteemed American poets writing today. One is impressed by his immersion in the widest of poetic traditions, resulting in flexibly measured lines, together with strikingly capacious metaphors, that often lead us to profound revelations about our human vagaries and contradictions. His is a patient, expansive mind that probes history, memory, place, and time with an august keenness into impermanence and mutability (that "gray flux [of] life"). Indeed, Tobin's art is one that steadies "the unsteady stave of lines to where they thread." Not only is he a gifted writer of the sonnet, but his mastery of the poetic sequence is breathtaking, especially evident in "Homage to Bartolomé de Las Casas" where he inhabits the friar's voice with extraordinary sensitivity and insight into his transformation from colonizer to apostle of the Indies. A second sequence, "The Narrows," is another tour de force that examines the Irish Diaspora, both historically and personally, making the strands and fragments of memory into an exquisite tapestry of the American experience.

—Orlando Ricardo Menes

Dusk, Empire

New and Selected Poems

1987–2024

Also by Daniel Tobin

Poetry

Where the World Is Made (1999)
Double Life (2004)
The Narrows (2005)
Second Things (2008)
Belated Heavens (2010)
The Net (2014)
From Nothing (2016)
Blood Labors (2018)
The Mansions (2023)

Translation

The Stone in the Air: A Suite of Forty Poems from the German of Paul Celan (2018)

Chapbook

Gloss Arias I: From the Distances of Sleep (2025)

Criticism

Passage to the Center: Imagination and the Sacred in the Poetry of Seamus Heaney (1999)
Awake in America (2011)
On Serious Earth (2019)
The Odeon (2025)

Editor

Light in Hand: Selected Early Poems of Lola Ridge (2007)
Poet's Work, Poet's Play: Essays on the Practice and the Art (2007, with Pimone Triplett)
The Book of Irish American Poetry from the Eighteenth Century to the Present (2008)
To the Many: The Collected Early Works of Lola Ridge (2018)

Dusk, Empire

New and Selected Poems

1987–2024

Daniel Tobin

Four Way Books
Tribeca

Library of Congress Cataloging-in-Publication Data

Names: Tobin, Daniel, author
Title: Dusk, empire : new and selected poems, 1987-2024 / by Daniel Tobin.
Other titles: Dusk, empire (Compilation)
Description: New York : Four Way Books, 2026.
Identifiers: LCCN 2025027267 (print) | LCCN 2025027268 (ebook) |
ISBN 9781961897762 trade paperback | ISBN 9781961897779 ebook
Subjects: LCGFT: Poetry
Classification: LCC PS3570.O289 D87 2026 (print) | LCC PS3570.O289 (ebook)
LC record available at https://lccn.loc.gov/2025027267
LC ebook record available at https://lccn.loc.gov/2025027268

This book is manufactured in the United States of America and printed on acid-free paper.

Four Way Books is a not-for-profit literary press. We are grateful for the assistance we receive from individual donors, public arts agencies, and private foundations including the New York State Council on the Arts, a state agency.

We are a proud member of the Community of Literary Magazines and Presses.

Contents

From *Belated Heavens* (2010)

From *The Net* (2014)

From *Blood Labors* (2018)

Coda

Notes

A NOTE

I have chosen not to include any work from the three book-length poems of *The Mansions,* in part because the poems are composed of individual cantos within the sections of each book.The books themselves, in turn, are movements within the larger design of the whole trilogy. Also, I have not included poems from *The Stone in the Air*, my sequence of forty versions from the work of Paul Celan. I feel it is appropriate to let both larger-scale sequences stand alongside, rather than within, the present volume. The like is true of the chapbook *From the Distances of Sleep*. Finally, *The Narrows*, a mural in verse, has been pared down considerably for reasons of space, and two poems, "A Green Road in Clare" and "The Line," have been added here to complete the whole. I hope the interested reader will turn to these works as companions to the present selection of nearly forty years.

Dusk, Empire

New and Selected Poems 1987–2024

Dusk, Empire: New Poems

The times are evil, the times are troubled, that's what people say. Let us live good lives, and the times are good. We ourselves are the times. Whatever we are like, that's what the times are like.

Augustine of Hippo, *Sermons*

A Quiet Evening in Shock and Awe

A retrospect

Tonight, the local symphony
    of sirens, gunshots, car alarms
dissipates in a swale of wind
    beyond the blinds' impending swarm

of talking heads that babble on
    to hype the heave of history,
while bomb bursts blast the foreign town
    to mangles of stone and steel and dust.

Meanwhile, the mission of the leaves
    accomplishes in winter's dearth
an inference, golden, that trumps the freeze
    and makes a manifest of earth

that lifts above each sponsored lie
    (our word is lesser than we guessed)
like wingbeats in a prodigal's sty—
    the brute rejoicings of the blest.

Monopoly, 1973

Dug-out walls. Sawhorse and spades in waiting,
hung on hammered nails or piled neatly.
Dank smell of dampened humus weathering.

That plywood shelf tabled to concrete blocks
was our summer game board lazy afternoons.
Sanita, Sullivan, Greco and me—our stacks

of play money ranged in parceled colors.
One of us a thimble. One of us a hat.
One of us a dog. One of us a race car.

Roll the dice. Circle the square in turn,
accruing as we could the mock real estate,
Baltic or Boardwalk, skid row or demesne,

taking what we could where chance landed us,
jackpot or jail, the saving cash for passing Go,
planting our plastic houses and hotels

so one could supplant the rest one by one
for unpaid rent: *Five-hundred Snapagoneegoes*!
For today let's say it was Sullivan,

and such was the lingo of his currency,
as one by one indeed we settled up
until there was nothing left to settle for,

the way OPEC decided to embargo crude,
and what was shaping up to be "a gilt-edged year"
blundered to stagflation and the usual greed.

While Sanita's father buried himself
under a blown-out engine block, and Greco's sat
upstairs, a few lawns mowed and no work left,

and mine, desk-bound, checked the time,
and Sullivan's climbed another humming pole
up through the trees to the power lines

that stretched away like a receding script
as his son exulted in the cellar dark
who'd ground his good friends blithely to the dirt.

The White Road

I am walking along the dazzling ruin of a road I knew
When I was fourteen, summer, and the days stretch out
Like the road itself, or like that song about a road heading
Somewhere far off into the unseen and the one walking,
Caminante, no hay camino, knows he's come upon his life
Rising up to him in white quartz macadam and heat-haze.
Along the slapdash shoulder a few almost-teenage boys
Are shaving down stalks of goldenrod in afternoon sun,
The better to whip the heads off weeds, or whip each other
Before nothing much calls them to loiter off elsewhere
To Grossi's Junkyard or the Shale Pit or, today, saunter
The dirt lane down to the Lower Lake where in three years
Dante Tedeschi will fashion a ramp out of cast-off
Plywood and scrap, aiming to accomplish something
No one has dared before—to tear down Heart Attack Hill
Past Hendershot's house, in full view of the ball courts,
The beach where Patty Curiale, all glistening skin and breasts
In her string bikini, suns her blonde self, her feet dangling
From the wooden dock; or she's out on the raft readying
To dive with a lithe grace into the unseeable-into murk
Of the middle of that dammed-up pond we called a lake—
Which is, approximately, the medium into which Dante aims
To take flight, hauling from the hilltop at top speed
Toward the ramp he's sturdied beside the bridge, as if
He was on his father's Harley and not some souped-up
Almighty Schwinn, its raised handles, its roll bar,
The flared banana seat, as though this were a road bike
And he some mythical Easy Rider twisting the hand grips
To gun it beyond sound or sense into a catalytic future.

We called him Boone, even our fathers called him Boone,
Our mothers, arrayed in neon polyester like kitsch
Statuary outside their jerry-built summer houses—
Coolers of beer and whisky sours all evening long
Under citronella torches, weekend parties that made

The rounds from porch to patio while their children
Wandered off. Here he comes now, Dante aka Boone,
With his incongruous swagger and coke-bottle glasses,
Twirling a cut-down stick in his left hand that he now
Pretends is a Louisville Slugger he summons to swing,
A dead-pull hitter blithely turning on the invisible,
The fastball deposited somewhere deep in the vetch
Across the sweltering pitch and glitter of the White Road.
His laugh was a kind of rapid-fire staccato, shuttling
Between a case of hiccups and a howitzer, unfettered,
Pure enjoyment admixed to a purer derision.
Like when, playing chess on Garrity's lawn, he'd stare
Expressionless at his opponent's spread of forces, pawns
Advancing, bishops slicing slantwise over the squares,
And in no time their Queen taken, King checkmated,
And it shot up uncontrollable, infiltrating the canopy,
The shade trees sheltering the picnic table, echoing
Off the rusted shed: that impishly jocular spattering
Of genius immodestly, no surprise to us, surprising
Itself once again with its own manic and rarified life.
Always he attained whatever he desired, slaughter
On the game board, sliding catches in left-center
On Power's Field, even the soft-limbed Patty of dreams.
He'd take her nightly to Schuman's porch, the house
Disused, or abandoned, the rest of us pent and waiting
With the unkempt fevers of our bodies that longed
To trespass beyond their churning borders. Like a spoon
Slipping into honey, he'd say, letting his simile float
In the air awhile among us like a fraying wing of smoke,
The blazon of his carnal knowing.

He was first to go,
The buzz coming by phone one winter evening
After those summers had disbanded to intimations
Of more necessary longings, for jobs, for departures,

The bullet passing clean through his skull at a sister's
Wedding, the trigger pulled by the groom's hand.
What he had done or said, none of us would come
To know, though all of us could hear inside
That rapid-fire laugh, haughty, untamable, and saw
His shambling, self-assured walk as in a heatwave
Off the White Road, Dante alias Boone, in saddle
On his Schwinn wheeling breakneck from on high
Down Heart Attack in the mind's would-be perpetual
Now, hair flying, pot-holes' loose gravel be damned,
Down to where the rigged ramp rose upward above
The waiting lake, our crowd of bored numb-nuts cheering
As bike and rider flew treacherously up into the air
And out beyond the shore, and disappeared—circlets
Of waves radiating out like visible ticks from a clock face,
Slowly softening into nothing one by one by one
As we waited for the quick-eyed, impudent head to rise.

Drainpipe

Gravel scrabble summer storms wasted down
off the shoulder to a three-foot-wide mouth,
the cast tube fitted snugly underground

before they graded it over, stone and pitch
smoothed under the roller's unrelenting weight—
that's where the boys stood, as if a hatch

yawned its slim passage to another world
that glowed down the tunnel at the far end—
a bright, white portal to the other side.

One of them, the bravest, the crazy one,
crouched low to grabble the road-wash away
where the dark gaped, corrugated, prone.

His friends milled above while he, unwavering,
(only a shadow of what could happen
calculated inside the eye's glazed chamber),

sloped his shoulders inward and ducked under
where coolness tempered on him like a squall
and blown grit and pebbles littered his hands,

and his shins, naked, felt the remnant *slur*
of whatever flowed in and flurried through
that soldered casing of what comes and goes.

And now midway maybe he felt something
in the pit of himself crawling, a blackness,
like a body thrown back to its beginning,

or an old man hauling on elbows and knees
along the floor, unable to walk, hauling,
he wants to crawl out of his own body—

that waste tube, that slurry gate—until all
concentrates into the white portal ahead,
the steel-encased lives ramrodding above,

the boy hunching forward now and setting
on day, his grave, quickening grovel when
he comes out from the leaden into light,

the waiting faces of others in the open…

The Calls

All the dead on the answering machine
live on in old technology, the now before
what called them culled them as it goes.

From where the blinking numbers shine
they speak, as from some taped eternity
where the past repeats like sea whispers

out of an empty shell, their trace a hush—
you'd have them conjure each lost face.
A cousin from cancer's bottomless well

forever calls to say she's fine; that friend,
car crash, jokes from his unbroken sleep
until the vanished are raised inerasable.

Still the pinwheel makes its timely round
while the handset hangs on silently.
Replay, again, that lover's voice: *It's just me.*

Herald

The birds, common sparrows, must like the bush
flaming autumn yellow in the neighbor's yard.
Not the kind to trace a flyway, the weather warming,
they home here awhile, flickering among the leaves
like rogue leaves themselves, browned, readying.

And the cat must like the birds. For hours it seems
he's crouching at the fringe, not purring, but bracing
to what can only be an electric hum—his body
attentive, hot-wired for the strike.
                                        Along the fence
my neighbor's fastened brazen stars, a brazen sun—
summer's faux adornments, congenial emblems,

like the pastoral metaphor my student ventured
for his mother, dead, the disease withering her
limb by limb, until her last breath dissembled
to plumes of drifted smoke—*My mother, a garden*…
his lines winnowing contrapuntal down the page.

Unseasonal, the real sun embellishes the beds
raked over, bagged, cat unaccountably gone.
Now, from inside, the whole bush is shaking,
a frantic chorus, as though it were about to speak.

Dusk, Empire

A red-tailed hawk in a coat of folded wings
perches on the peak of my neighbor's roof,
in its talons the clasped prey, some mammal
or other—some pest one should be glad
has met its master, though it's bad form
to say so, even if this most majestic gauge
of power clarifies the wider grip of things.

Another neighbor now comes to the fence,
he appears on reconnaissance for a closer look,
his black binoculars refracting the late light
of fall he's seeing through, as if he were
surveying some enemy hidden in desert hills,
or storming in formation along a newsreel
from our unlost past. The bird cares nothing

for our curiosity, or is it our wonder as one
angles his phone to capture that profile's
utter watchfulness, this strayed herald
from altogether elsewhere, suddenly gone—
while the cat patrols his usual border,
and jays commence their bottlerocket screeches,
and under its eave a pigeon's plaintive *mur mur*
sounds like someone with a hand over his mouth.

In the Greencroft

For Rondell, Virginia, 1986

Under the pan where the order simmers
low flames lap to the rhythm of your hand,
short orders only, your only command,
and up front—the clubroom, posh with diners.

You know your place, lot, the lay of land
that shuts your face behind two swinging doors.
Under the pot where the order simmers
low flames lap to the rhythm of your hand

that would lift to strike whoever strays
into your torrid zone. At the stove you stand
deferred, while orders rote inside your pan
sizzle like cravings to settle old scores.
Under the pan where the order simmers
low flames lap to the rhythm of your hand.

Fable of the Alternative Fact

A slick slug comes to glisten in the ear.
It slides where once a wary owl would perch
to scan what seemed an overlay of earth—
figural owl in a figural ear

flown or fallen, or so it would appear,
as though it were the emblem of our dearth,
this slick slug come to glisten in the ear.
It slides where once a wary owl could perch,

then into the very nadir of the year,
the zero core, absolute, sans rebirth.
What *In Hoc Signo* lifts above its church?
What acumen betrays the words we hear?
A slick slug comes to glisten in the ear.

Method

Limb by limb they take its freight of leaves,
the saw's raw buzzing revving every branch
like a motorbike's wild, abrasive amp
cramming bandwidths through the ear's cave.
The tree's little more than a post now,
and now (post the parenthetical
carting away of the severed canopy
that swayed awhile during lambent hours
when the gold buds had broken open
and splayed deltas of foliage hung
newly pendant above the yard) nothing
much arrows into sky, the lopped
portions just pithy zeros on the trunk,
what flared greenly bent for the shredder
then shot in the truck's compliant bed.
Now, with the strict posture of a monk,
or the iron acquiescence of a Giacometti,
it falls at the textbook cleaving, block
by tapered block, until only stump is left—
one widening inconvenient life reaching
where it would.
                                        Days later, a glaze appears
on the floored butte, pooling there, sap's
sugar coating, unrisen, textured like shellac.
Still, all around this sawdust squall drifts,
the high sun blazing, lightened, relentless.

In a Public Pool

"The body went unnoticed for four days..."
Reuters

The woman at the bottom swims in place,
arms lifting again in fluid dusk, then
lowering with the water's blent embrace.
She dandles there as though in slow motion
while all around scissor legs of children
in the turbid stillness where they race
like fleet figures of a blemished ocean,
and no one stoops to face her secret face.

Giddy players at the slide. Two boys chase
each other through the murk, and splash for fun
a klatch of screaming girls. A baby wades,
not motherless, at the edge. The woman's gone
where *now* has turned oblivious to *then*
as young bodies, brave with flailing arms, trace
the trackless line where a moment had been,
but no one stoops to face her secret face.

Where is she headed in the clouded waste
of this vague medium, amniotic to the bone
with everything, like her, to be erased—
intended to be, here, or merely thrown?
Is there some depth that can quench, quicken,
and she span her arms to a finer distance
(the womb inside the world inside the Hidden)
where something stoops to touch her secret face?

In time there are shouts. Men with waders run
to plumb the shallows, as crowds—no disgrace—
watch them raise her bluing legs into the sun
before they stoop to face a secret face.

Anthem

Meleagris gallopavo

Through the backyard of a shuttered home
the birds have come, an almost emblem
of the young Republic, more respectable
Ben Franklin believed than the bald eagle

that was like, he said, a man who lived
by sharping and robbing, a rank coward,
driven from the districts by little more
than sparrows; perched up in dead trees or,

too lazy to fish for himself, off to pursue
the self-won catch of the diligent osprey,
snatching it from hatchlings in their nest—
"Is this not the perfect token of injustice?"

Not like these, the hen with its fledglings
scanning the remnant grass to scavenge
nuts and seeds, heads lifted, is it proudly,
as they catch you watching them, wary

with their onyx eyes, but nonchalant,
legs in the attitude of a ballet dancer's
to take the slightest step? Just weeks ago,
one might have seen behind a window

children's faces in a room given over,
eyes wide to the roving interlopers,
their coppery feathers garnet-dusted
in sunlight, the belated saurian heads

daubed with a pink and blue impasto,
as if Pollock'd spattered dollops for show,
or they'd just frittered onto the canvas
unknowing. Unlike holiday carcasses,

the big, snooded toms are brighter still:
paint-splashed totem faces. The flush wattles
hang like blurry fritillaries below the beak,
and should you seem a threat they'll strike—

a bird of Courage, Mr. Franklin believed,
who wouldn't fear to seize, being native
to this continent, some British grenadier
who'd flagrantly transgress the farmyard.

All spent, nearly, it's good they have returned,
the conifer forests thinned, to this urban
habitat, the emptied house, the family gone—
the dream some contractor will purchase for a song.

The Door

John 3:17

Those two at the door,
mild-eyed, chosen,
carry their booklets
and crosses in bags
to save me who needs
saving, *Through his wounds
the world is healed.*
And I'm for healing,
though what follows,
talk of second deaths,
pits, eternal anguish,
transports me to nights
like the last, long moans
beyond our garden,
mewling—the predator
at its prey—the way
a siren can wind down
streets away to gunshot
or stroke, some portal
to wreckage, between
those slow sounds
of pain a life draining—
and that low, reverent
growl from the throat
at the throat: not good,
not bad, just the wheel's
mastery under a moon's
blind eye. And me
past midnight listening
as I listen now,
O my discomfiting
comforters, turning
from me having given
what you could give.

Little Hallows

Door to door the costumed children come
to sweetly demonize the block
with their one demand, before they flock
en masse to the next, then head for home

where, later, the TV news will rage
with un-true believers, their latest prey
soaked alive in gas and set aflame.
They watched him flail and writhe inside his cage

until the flesh charred crisply into ash
and the bones crackled through. Eyes clear,
they filmed the screaming one, and cheered,
then carried out the body with the trash.

Above, the sky appears another skin,
pure blue, unmasked, where like a screen
closing over, the mackerel clouds descend
to bar us here, where all souls are shut in,

and a beech's coffer of fake doubloons
blazing in declining sun
showers its coinage one by one
to litter the pure effacement of the wind.

The Combatants

> Choose your enemies carefully, because
> you will become like them.
> René Girard

What lame god will fashion them on his shield
As during those great, grim mythic seasons,
The bodies stacked high as a harvest-yield?

Sky drones. Clashing switches: missiles wield
Their fleet nemeses on fleshly elisions.
What lame god will fashion them on his shield

That captures, sheer rigor, the raving field,
The gorged mortis of the hater's reasons?
The bodies, stacked high as a harvest-yield,

Extenuate in pretense, blood annealed,
Flung with the surfeit of love's brave treasons.
What lame god will fashion them on his shield

So pixel-perfect for the spectacle's appeal
It clinches history's tangle of intrusions.
These bodies stacked high as a harvest-yield

Look skyward, gazing dimly through a veil
That falls like ash before the ardent legions.
What lame god will fashion them on his shield?
The bodies stack high as a harvest-yield.

Triumphs and Laments

After William Kentridge,
Triumphs and Laments, pollution erasure, Tiber River, Rome

As though these words were shadows sprayed
across a wall of travertine
such figures resurrect the scene
blanched to presence on this page—

stone, really, the white river wall
stenciled with attributes of moss
and merely human detritus,
its negative space colossal.

Here within this running frieze
Romulus murders again his twin,
soldiers behead barbarians
as a saint sighs in ecstasy.

Here lovers in a fountain splash
wildly for La Dolce Vita,
as the broken march, defeated,
to where the ghetto flies to ash.

Bruno, too, lashed to his pyre
upside down, his eyes set
on infinities, mouth clamped shut,
stokes the verities of empire.

Forms, in this smoky procession,
move cinematically on
toward some ever-far beyond;
a glum fade will be their passion.

Are they awash in Plato's Cave
played there from the glowing embers,
That Which I Do Not Remember
signed above their hopeless way?

Deliberate fingers of the air
blacken slowly all we see,
as with spot-lit graffiti
they issue all to disappear.

Meanwhile, in some stray niche of time,
Michelangelo, blind, old,
glides his hand along the fold
of a statue's marble thigh,

and recollects the ideal age
when his chisel found the seam
to the body inside the dream,
the stone, the blow, the rock, the rage.

Gleninagh

An féar gorta ("the hungry man," "the hungry grass")

The last stile opens
on lashing wind and rain—a storm
born on the Atlantic,

heaving the high moor
where we walk, bone-soaked and blinkered,
snooded in our hoods.

We'd followed along
a world's edge, the green road's ledge
from gold strand

to Blackhead, limestone
like frozen whitecaps in the scutch,
a clean-washed moonscape

where pavements rise
to ridge and ring-fort, the kestral's
eyrie of tilt and waft.

Below us, new farms
leaned fondly into the bay, livestock
dawdling the verges

marking drystone walls
of remnant fields, beside them buried
in hawthorn and hazel

the hovels of the lost,
the starving lying where they fell, heaved
into mass graves, the rest

shipped out, others
hunkered, scratching it out: the few, fittest,
or were they the fiercest?

On this wide saddle
between two terraced mountains, high above
that tower house staring

blankly at the waves,
we bow our heads toward un-hungry grass,
eying the way marks,

and bowing lower still
to side-blowing wind, side-blown rain—this
light touch of the merciless.

We See a Kestrel Hover Over

the jigsaw lineaments of clint and grike,
terraces worn clean by rain and gale—

this remnant shelf inched by slippages
from equatorial to northern ridges

before the elk arrived in slow hoards,
foragers, hunters, Neolithic herds—

the human increase of unhuman wind.
The bird rides there impossibly, a mind

awake to air's each shifting modicum,
wings spread out, a buoyant equilibrium—

more through than in each thermal blow
buffeting headland and storm beach below,

as the raptor, tantalizingly still, looks
it appears, down on us, our near bucklings

over stone—we who live otherwise
not indistinct, our consequence of days

quickening. Above: a moonscape *slieve*,
a fort's scant ring of stones; and under: cave

on cave, a hidden system. This bird holds.
In the wind our windbreakers snap like ropes.

With the Gift of a Feather at Coole Park

Nothing left of the great house now
but these stuttering steps
leading nowhere,
a tearoom selling crepes,
day-trippers with their camera-ready phones
vaguely on the hunt for swans.

We walk again these sodden woodland trails
enwound like loosened twine,
attending viewpoints of the famed reserve.
Fields away, the M18
gouges its karstic scar to new estates
where the outer suburb starts.

Years ago, the prospect of these woods
(or was it just our wants)
quickened us. The tracts of felled or fallen trees
spurred by rot, acid rains,
offer vantage onto lowland rills
before those fossil hills.

At the lakeshore where the turlough floods,
a son—his father turned
aside to some distance in his mood
he holds apart—skips stones
ardently into the still waters
and the gray wash dimly stirs.

I would teach him how to choose the one,
judge its shape, its feel
along the angled finger and the palm,
to see the sightline clear
until along a mirror's windless sky
it skipped to his wide eye

the arrowed ripples spreading on the brim.
We turn away instead
to find in scrabble this one feather,
the bird flown from its shed.
It could be a child's quill, pure white,
at the frill the faintest brush of night.

The Lesson

Or else swoon to death, the young poet wrote,
        though these in the seminar's steadfast room
appear to want little or none of it,
        however coddlingly the professor prods.
They are the poet's age at death, or almost,
        but do not find "relatable" these words
composed by one who knew his passion hopeless—
        especially the *sleepless Eremite*,
belonging to another world and time,
        and even his *fair love's ripening breast*
conjures only suspect looks, withering stares,
        or now and then a tolerating nod.
Of course, they must assume their own bright stars
        will rise aloft some digital empyrean

forever new, as each one makes their way
        to find fulfillment's *human shores*, one hopes,
and not some desolate attic. It's the boy
        behind who's turned to something out beyond
the glazing, at the leafless Common,
        announcing to all the falcon's sudden plummet
in the haunt outside, the squirrel pinned,
        that beak going tenderly at neck and throat.
Will he fathom what the prey beholds
        from its hazing scrim of consciousness? The bird
lifts, soon enough, above the whitened patch
        of ground, a frozen *mask*, receding veil
of walks and trees, this restless cityscape,
        those wings tilting to an even paler sky.

Hunter Gatherers

All this morning in the newly winnowed trees
squirrels are chirring, as though each one inside
had a miniature fan rotating urgently,
the impossibly rapid rpms of their language.

I can almost see through the thinned-out screen
of leaves a few tails waving like metronomes—
the wind lifting them? Or are they plumes, the nibs
of scribes at their appointed work, glossing

the margins, fearful the raiders will come again?
One, I watch him from my deck with the cats,
flies in a wild prodigious leap to the pole
(Be careful of the power box!) to tightrope across

this unsteady stave of lines to where they thread
under the eave. And up he hoists himself now
into the gutter, into the hole he's probably chewed
into the frame, into the attic, to fatten his store.

If they could the cats would have him, each perched
below on the rail, easy regression, paws quieted,
sly on savannah grass. Who is that nearby, beside
the umbrella thorn, newly upright with the rest,

ready to fan out like the branches above them,
getting ready with their flints to dis-limb the world?
Ripples like invisible arrows flit across the plain.
Is now the setting out? Where are we all going?

Swallowtail

For Bella Bond

Slowly as soundlessly in its unknowing,
what the driven thing must hunger for
is love's white noise—a latent faring
writhe along the leafage's flagrant green;
green, too, this wending, callow, creaturely,
unheedful in its patient haste of eyes
watchful beside the deck's complacent cage
of spindles. So, we lift the cat tenderly
indoors, our sweet, beloved predator
hard-wired for the hunt, and lean in closer.

Tiger, zebra-like the transverse lashings,
each a spray of onyx gold-licked at the edge,
its ten segments a kind of plump machine,
the crest, it seems, mulling its tiny lea.
Beauty, Augustine knew, was a manifold
diversity—sky and earth and sea—no less
this gradual ascendant likewise fueled
by desire, even *the smallest bulk that moves*,
though *the earthly body pulls toward earth,*
its blindly pulsing climb the flesh's goad.

Just so, at the would-be saint's retreat,
the whole company gathered to attend
how the chopped portions of a centipede
inched across a tablet of their own accord.
Is the beast's soul also divisible, one worm
disproving the venerable Plato's doctrine,
its immaterial nature hacked to living bits?
Thagaste lay behind him, and Rome, Milan,
his intended life, nameless loves, his lust,
all dust going to dust under a fig tree,

his pent longing in the garden a tumult
of the will—*The mind commands the hand*

to move, yet mind is mind and hand is body.
Ahead, there is Ostia, his mother's death,
that quickened time in a further garden
where, he confessed, *our minds were lifted*
to inexhaustible abundance, so the flesh,
the radiant light of this physical world,
ceases to matter compared with eternity; then years
unhomely in his African home, penned in

by duties, penning his peregrine *Civitas Dei*—
lawsuits, letters, a slow gutting of heresies,
his world hung *where moth and rust consume.*
Larval, what may yet emerge imago
slides a little as we lift it leaf and all
from its camouflage along the potted herbs
to rest it somewhere deeper in our garden,
somewhere, where, in peace, it can spin itself
into a patient sack, its silken matrix
of transfiguration. Once, I saw one

hooked like a frosted ornament on its branch,
the chrysalis growing slowly transparent
before the new body loosens to take wing.
When, this spring, they found the little girl,
faceless, decomposed, she had washed ashore,
dumped in a duffle in the harbor.
So they scanned her skull to resurrect her,
enhanced the image with digital grace
until we saw her as she must have been,
looking at us, past us, through pixelated light.

"It was her time to die," the killer offered
months later—her mother's lover, her mother
also harrowing her, her few years living—
"possessed by demons," they said, the pair's

high school photos discordant on the news.
All things draw toward some image of true joy,
Augustine believed, and believed likewise
the dead have bodies, composed of spirit,
their given flesh restored and glorified
where *not a single hair of the head will perish*.

The damned, too, have bodies, living, he held,
the way a salamander sustains in fire,
burning forever without loss of substance—
though evil is just deficiency, a turning
toward separateness, our region of unlikeness
in which *mortal life passes away like smoke*
and *the moment life begins it starts to die*:
the nothing in things that pretends to be,
pretends in division and butchery
until grief *torments like a worm in timber*,

and each thing tending toward eternal life
or eternal death. And our swallowtail?
Down in the canopy among the hostas
and sweet fennel, along a fence's rusted
diamond, it has wound its world around
itself, has been drawn to that going
inside as by a loadstone's lure beyond
the given, *miracle of miracles the world*
itself, though there is no safe place,
the saint recalled, but in the uncreated.

And still the bodies go, particle by particle,
to their peace as into an olive press.
And above, the firmament still stretches
like a skin, while below we remain
a problem to ourselves, while time distends
endlessly, it seems, cruelly, to what end?

The saint, imago, and murdered girl
must know, as if her name, *Bella*, Beauty,
were the all-in-all that calls to everything
soundlessly as slowly in our unknowing.

The Ruin

After the Anglo-Saxon

These wondrous wall-works, fate's ways wrecked them—
  the buildings blasted, colossal labors crumbled,
roof-beams raining down, and tallest towers toppled
  with each ashen shaft. Frost on every frieze,
the wind-shelters, shattered, were desecrated by age.
  Ground's grip seized the grave-hoven makers
in earth's firm grasp, everyone, ever, gone for good.
  And so, they run red, the lichen-mortared halls,
high and wide, reign after reign withstanding storms,
  until they too were all doggedly driven down.
Though muddled in muck, some spirit still persists
  of the keenly crafted work, each ring wrought
as to unfurl a fortress, this one so finely fashioned
  it would gird together the whole of what's-gone.
They must have been brilliant, the buildings and baths,
  raucous crowds clamoring in rooms to drink
under soaring ceilings, until what comes scuttled all.
  All over the fighters fell, plague days followed
to trample every remnant who would take a stand,
  the sacred places shuddered to their footings—
this realm laid waste. The ones who would raise it
  also sank into clay. So, from somber domes
of vaulted wooden rings, the shed tiles scattered
  their scarlet: eminence into mounds, shards
where once gathered throngs, glamorous, glittered,
  splendidly adorned, glad of good fortune,
well-flush with wine and self-wonder, their wealth
  flaunted like medallions plundered from war—
the gold, the silver, the precious jewels and stones,
  no city out of reach of this realm's radiance.
Where a steaming stream welled, spreading widely,
  the stone hall stood, all the baths bubbling,
and its walls enwound them like a bright womb
  that held and heated them at the very heart.
All was as it was. Let it run on, this hot current

over pale-worn stone, like ink disappeared
from scraps of a blistered page illegible in the ruin.
This, too, in effacement, is no negligible thing.

The Sand Painting

Each intricate, lovely thing will be erased.
Worldly hands banish what the worlds regard.

Worldly hands vanish from the world's regard
Believing they had scored the world in stone.

The self-adoring atoms whirl in stone.
This brightly colored dome reclines in sand

And casts the four directions into sand,
And centers the very wind with patient dust—

Conjured intimations of the ancient dust.
Someone labored faithfully grain by grain

Knowing all would scatter grain by grain,
Or wear away, as air destroys the rock.

What is that joyous singing inside the rock,
Though each intricate, lovely thing will be erased?

From *Where the World is Made* (1999)

Time is for man, not man for time.

The Cloud of Unknowing

Divinity dwells under Seal –

Emily Dickinson

The Clock

Bored with plastic armies,
he climbs onto the parlor loveseat
and watches the wide expression of the clock.
He doesn't know what time is,
doesn't know how in no time
those numbers will fill his days
the way water fills a bath
into which an exhausted man
lowers himself, not wanting to rise.
Sun and moon gaze back at him
from the glaze of the silver frame,
each with a human face,
his own face mirrored there.
Look closer, his mother says,
and you can see the small hand move.
And he leans closer now, steadied
in her arms, the hand a winded runner
lapped on the track. *That's hours*,
she says, *the big hand's minutes, the quick,*
seconds. And the boy fingers the pivot
anchoring them, his touch
stirs with the machine.
I'm older now, and now, and now. The gears
start to tick through every room of that house.

René Rilke

...everything is womb.
Rilke, "Eighth Duino Elegy"

Before Orpheus grew, a tree in your ear;
before angels terrified you into song;
before *Rainer*, you were *René*, the dress
blue as Mary's robes, blue of the mother,
your collar frilled under its weight of curls.
You were all she wanted you to be,

playing dolls behind the black screen painted
with dragons, under your family's cross.
And they come alive in your hands: father,
mother, all the griefs received like toys,
until you lose the bliss of one who stays
forever in the womb. But weren't griefs there,

too, palpable as shared blood? And the fears.
From all you'll become you'll glance back
to discover who you are, for one purpose:
to be born again out of yourself:
doting girl, bitter cadet. A friend dies
in childbirth and she has your own face.

Born to death like a star to its constellation,
you will learn to leave the given name behind—
Everything is womb. Now you rise in the light
of a Prague parlor, *puer*, to prayers,
to a woman's voice calling the length
of the long hallway, and never turn back.

My Uncle's Watch

"Bist du Jude? Bist du Jude?" the SS
officer repeated, like a schoolteacher
menacing a slow pupil, the camp for POWs
a train ride from Dachau. "Nicht Jude,"
my uncle told him: "I'm not a Jew,"
his whole body braced while the cold eyes
probed the face of the watch he bought
on Hester Street before the war,
the jeweler's name still etched on the case
behind the steadily turning hands.

Christmas, my eleventh year, a quarter century later,
I watched his unbroken body
ease into the big Queen Anne chair
in my parents' house, the family crowded round,
the creche a tattered barracks under the tree.
He told how his captor twisted the watch
once around his finger,
then tossed it lightly in his lap,
an act, I know now, of unbounded mercy,
given Himmler's boast—"I say who is a Jew."

That was the year of the other impossibilities:
men walking on the moon, my team winning the pennant,
the bishop's question weighing on me like a threat
before my Confirmation. Come Easter,
the tall nun would enter the classroom,
black gown trailing to her nobbled shoes,
her face framed like a mask
inside the peaked hood, and fire another:
"Who of you would give yourselves as ransom
for the rest if the Nazis came here now?"

No one answered, regimented behind our desks,
but I heard my friends' jeers of "Christ-killer" explode

from the schoolyard to the synagogue across the street,
the nuns' veiled slurs, the neighbors' brusque "Cheap as a Jew,"
and saw myself a little Jew-Christ marched alone
to the gas chamber—Christ of the ashen-haired comforter,
Christ of the lampshade—forgetting that God
is no hero, but a child for whom others are killed,
so my uncle's watch could tick on his un-slashed wrist
in time without end and without redemption.

Boethius in Downstate

It's impossible to say why he keeps coming back,
so out of place in his consul's robes
torn and moth-eaten through centuries
of wandering what he called "this dull earth"—
tired old statesman, so far
from the burnish of eternal forms.
Now, like a lost boy stumbling on
an insistent path through some thick wood
he wakes to low moans, the beacon
of a television dazing the ward.
Here again are prisons where a man sits
in stained pajamas, cheeks sunken, spittle
glazing his stubbled chin; where a woman,
brain blighted like a walnut from within,
her housedress shredded by manic fingers,
stares as through the bars of her name.
The tube's glow throws a patina on their faces,
on the face of this philosopher who witnesses,
via satellite, the overthrow of the Good
in the fate of newsworthy refugees,
and the newest Goth mugs for the camera,
pats the head of the young hostage
whose parents, half a continent away,
must accept the sham as consolation...
Pride, honor, power, fame, sweet husk
of the body: for him every desire
withers to chaff in the mind's vise.
"To be anything but what I am"—a crab
scuttling through primeval muck; a wolf
tearing at its prey; an earthworm, slow angel,
bearing the stunned flesh to resurrection.
"Divine Sophia, my physician, you who see
beginning and end, who judge why the fortunes
of evil men flourish like gardens nourished
on richest loam, wipe this cloud of mortal things

from my eyes." And once again, as long ago,
a pear tree blazes up at him, the wind
already alive with the scent of fruit
to be gathered, of the fruit that will fall.

A Hunger

Tuam, Co. Galway

The farmer comes home late from the pub
his one evening free from work,
and finds what he feared, the heifer sick,
one hoof jutting from the straining rump,
the other turned back inside the womb—
as if the calf had lost its way,
nature itself unsure of the path.

It's no miracle, as he rolls his sleeve,
then plunges his arm, elbow deep, into the cow,
shifts the limb, a difficult gear, into place.
Now, he tightens the knotted rope around both,
and pulls until the shocked face emerges,
then spreads the opening wider, his hands
bristling with blood and water,
while the beast drones its low, unhuman cry.

Mastery is nothing but perfection of habit,
years on an unwanted farm, nursing cows,
nursing the mother who begged him to stay,
sentencing him to his blank inheritance,
until what tumbles into straw is an afterthought,
the moment spilling into its absence—
What I do is not done out of love;
in such loneliness I carry my dead.

Later, after the mother licks the new calf clean
and it starts to hobble on its spindly legs,
he will guide it to the tit, the dumb mouth
sucking anything, even the bloody sac
that hangs deceptively behind the tail
and, if eaten, could kill.

Passages

1. *Man Caught in a Black Hole*

What is this sudden traveling-through
as if a train had left the station
without a lurch, but full-throttle,
into the whirr of absolute motion?

Surely, it's no one's journey but my own,
quickened to thought from the womb's nest;
I arrived nowhere like weed to garden,
a fugitive passion to the breast.

When I shut my lids: galaxies, worlds,
the dust of a million creations
composed into that shining blur
glimpsed first as my mother's face.

Wherever this tunnel opens
there'll be a man with my own eyes
staring at me like a sun
waked from space, about to die.

2. *Stylite*

Let the faithful
laud me
where I sit
above them,
growing thinner
each year,
an arrow straining
for the mark.
To me they bring

meat, fruits,
food for this
unwanted body: all
I would leave.
To them I give
this image: a man
so touched by God
he has become
the ascended
column, ruined
finger the flesh
juts to heaven.
Each night
it is the one
wound I see
opening
between stars;
each day the sun's
empty face
burns away
more of my own.
I would assume
that gaze
as those below
assume mine.
Not the ideal's
pure form,
but the unbearable
light inside.

If You Cut Your Finger, Bandage the Knife

After a sculpture by Joseph Beuys

If you cut your finger, bandage the knife.
If you stub your toe, rub the wall.
If, stumbling on a stone, you crack your skull,
with your last breath ask pardon of the pavement
for its ignominy at your feet, for its grace
in waking you. When the murderer comes,
don't feel sorrow for his childhood, for the victim
at his feet; instead, take pity on the gun,
ill-used, like a mother, whose hard-hearted children
never come back. In the torture chamber, don't preach
to the torturers, nor comfort the exhausted broken ones;
but pray to the implements—rack, scalpel, electrode—
who know better than lovers the simplicity of touch.
Raise your eyes, kneel before the button.
And should you ask *Of what am I certain?*
feel the wound, in front of you, opening in air
where the world is made, as in a womb.

From *Double Life* (2004)

The world is the closed door. It is a barrier.
And at the same time it is the way through.

Simone Weil

Homage to Bosch

All flesh is grass, and all the goodliness thereof
is as the flower of the field...
Isaiah 40:6

And it was done. The universe a clear ball
gathering dust on nothing's highest shelf,
its snows drifted to mists from which the earth
rises, *en grisaille*, to its first morning.
Rivers and valleys. Rolling hills. Mountains
quickened from the ash of their vanishing.
A landscape colorless, before memory,
pierced by a ray from the receding whirlwind.
Above, sad-faced, ringed by clouds, God opens
his *Summa*, book of judgment and of straw.

I.

Our procession filed through the opened gates
of the Prado, leaving behind
the guitarists, sword-sellers, bronze horsemen
of Madrid. Forty schoolboys,
faces daubed with acne, what did we know
about the provinces of art?
We'd have preferred the hotel pool, tapestries
of beach towels, bikinis,
bold impastos of the Ramblas, Torremolinos.
Through rooms of portraits, scions
of history, I shadowed like the town fool
who stumbles into a coronation.
Then, more fabulous than a roadside carnival:
The Garden of Earthly Delights—
swarms of nudes, drunk on the juice of berries
bigger than balloons, tumbling
in the soft grass among seeds of pomegranates,
enormous fish, shimmering
bubbles housing lovers, kingfishers, goldfinches
parading toward the cavalcade

(a bestiary turning back on itself like a serpent
    eating its own tail) circling
the central pool. Was this sin or innocence,
    to skinny-dip with dragonflies,
paddle downstream in an apple-boat, or don the head
    of an owl to dance flamenco?
The fifteen-year-old I awoke to the choices:
    on the left wing, the Garden,
Christ in the gesture of a healer taking Eve's hand,
    Adam looking on, his feet
touching the divine gown while behind them the Fountain
    of Life pours out its rivers.
And on the right, the furnace-city of Hell,
    like a photograph of Dresden;
musicians crucified on harps, an enthroned demon
    with a chamber-pot crown
defecating the damned into torment's cesspool.
    Only now, years later, do I see
in the background of Paradise that lion rending
    the carcass of a deer,
how it's mirrored in the monster who's turned
    into a macabre Tree of Knowledge,
the sharp limbs piercing the cracked eggshell of skin
    in which devils sit at table—
as if evil had fashioned a tavern in the guts…
    That summer drifts, *sfumato*,
in the haze of memory: the Prado, Toledo,
    Avila, Monserrat, a man
collared by soldiers on the line to Gibraltar,
    beaten senseless, dragged off.

II.

How plentiful the world is, a wagon piled to bursting
with its golden trove of hay, wheels wobbling
underneath, squeaking, the great load teetering
in every rut.

We parade it through harvest fields, imagining before us
towns untouched by plague, abuzz with a babble of markets,
revels uninspired by the feast days of saints—
a kingdom of our own.

For us, every day is Mardi Gras. We crowd the driven cart
in scarlet tunics, emerald buskins, royal robes,
pale turbans, homespun wools, muslins and silks
as we whirl ahead in our St. Vitus Dance.

We trundle like an army through leveled forests once rife
with deer, wild boar, the ghosts of extinct species,
while behind us lands spread out in shimmering haze
as on the third day of creation.

Lords, emperors, archbishops, kings, their pockets heavy
with the weight of tithes; knights mantled in armor
speckled with the blood of crusades; ruminant clerics,
all train in back, marking their lots like destiny.

Where a jigging burgher clutches his purse to his heart,
another pitches his ladder to the wain, hoping to climb
atop to where a courtier with lute serenades a maid.

Do they hear the song below, those tearing at the stack,
tearing at each other as they're crushed
beneath the wheels?

The feasters turn away, sweet smells exuding
  from the campground—a pig's head roasting on its spit,
  trout on poles awaiting flame, casks of wine...

Still, we progress in our exodus, riotous as the rabble
  who fashioned a golden calf.

And what if, human, we were blinded by such fullness,
  cajoled by subaqueous demons who would brandish our heads
  on pikes—who's to say our fate could be otherwise?

The saint crouches in reverence over his testament, prey
  for spirits who taunt him from an altar spread
  with bread and wine.

Or from the hollowed trunk of an oak the temptress calls
  his name, fingering herself, while flying fish,
  bird-boats, ascend infernal skies.

The sufferings of the damned and saved, how alike they are—
  as if the Almighty sharpened his blade for all equally,
  and the arms extended in universal blessing
  were only the austere gesture of some bitter judgment.

And so that faint glow on the horizon must be Utopia,
  earthly paradise, the torch-lights of the millennium
  and final consummation burning in the eyes of a thief
  who slits his brother's throat for a fistful of straw.

III.

In Carpentras the dead are rising,
    joined by angels,
stunned to ecstasy by the beneficence

of light that lifts them
into its tunnel, a blinding cornucopia.
Assumed, do they forget
the desecration of their bodies?
Or have they accomplished
in their passing what we cannot:
forgiveness,
even of unimaginable horror?
I cling to my wrongs—
how as a child I couldn't pull the wings
off butterflies,
at other's egging, but secretly wished
for the deaths
of those boys who'd surround me
after school, faces
turned into a canvas of leering masks;
or my own betrayals—
the friends outgrown, lovers left,
family denied.
Puffed as Midas who fingered all he saw
into gold,
I acclaim my ambition to exceed
and call it virtue,
the way a dandy admires his image
in a mirror.
Is this, then, goodness: the arm of a boy
suddenly gone limp
when, charged by hurt, he most desires
to strike?
Is that why so often the world appears
unbearable,
because what is most truly us—the part
that suffers—
can't free itself from the cramped room
we've furnished for it

in the remotest mansion of ourselves.
    In that barn,
the bewildered child accepts the gifts
    of this world,
while behind him on the torn plain
    crazed horsemen clash.
Too soon he'll wake to the nightmare
    of mocking faces
that crowd him till his own is obscured
    in the rush of torture,
the driven cross… I bear on my back
    the weight of my own skin.

Bones on the road. A wreckage of weapons.
In clear light killers tie their victim
to a tree as another man hunkers off,
abandoned to his dream of refuge.
There are lovers in meadows, pipers
in fields. And on a far hill a throng
gathers for an execution. Through this land
the wanderer passes, his staff edging back
a rabid dog… Empty One, Unnamable,
only by your command are we sustained.

Human

Omo Dei

Dante, spurred by divine love, saw
the letter M in the human face,
sockets of the penitent
hollowed to a script
that marked the Maker's signature,
and praised it, sky-written emblem of the just,
as he ascended Paradise.

But this near-noon, at millennium's end,
after a morning of pick-up ball,
the only signs I see are for
the fast-food dives
where I pull in under a golden arch
that announces to the world
BILLIONS SOLD. Do they mean what
or who? For lined up as we are
we could be a train of souls
undone by suspect appetites.

By now, I should be at ease
living *in the middest*, apart
from the sure path—the way
those ballplayers in the booth across
laugh it up after a game; or the way
that child, escaped from her father,
dances up the aisle with a joyful wail,
oblivious as a dervish, ignorant
of the looks her face begets;
and ignorant of the face
that wiseass makes behind her back,
like something out of Bosch,
while the whole booth bursts out laughing.

As she makes her way back up the rows
of plastic seats, her face appears
much older than her age, her eyes
too widely spread apart, as if clay
had been too hastily fixed, the form
miscast by some uncertain hand.
Now her father gathers her away
from the muted jibes and stares,
and those like me who turn aside
fascinated by some message
hidden among our scraps
of lunch, and carries her to play outside

where a clownish cop, his head
shaped like a hamburger,
his eyes pools of blistered paint,
stands guard over other, stranger beings.
And she climbs up with the same rapt screech
to wave at her father through the bars.

At the Egyptian Exhibit

Thou shalt have power over water, breathe air,
be surfeited with the desires of the heart...
from an Egyptian sarcophagus

How, you said, you used to sleep—the way
the mummy's hand flared awkwardly, twisted
just so, transposings of the quick and dead
made tractable behind glass. In his day:
tombs stocked full as bomb shelters, the soul
beaked and twittering over the body's haunts,
or casting off from rushes in the sun's boat.
What scares is how I see you, not cured, gaunt
as this shell, but a child curled in your bed,
your small hand in the shape of something gone
but for its remnant. As if someone wedded
these worlds as unalike as skin and stone.
Or as though the wind had stopped to trace
its image in the sphinx's disappearing face.

House-Hunting

Also, they have temples and sacred places in which
the gods really dwell, and they hear their voices
and receive their answers.
Plato, *Phaedo*

Our realtor reminds me of my freshman
philosophy teacher, a would-be Cagney
with mid-life spread filling out
the blue sport coat and gray pants.
As he flips through keys, small-talking,
dismissing all before finding the one
that clicks open the lock, I can almost see
Professor Azar leaning over his desk,
doing his best to sell forty blank stares
on the virtues of virtue.

Few of us cared
to get his ad hoc lectures salvaged
from dead air, Socratic jibes
fallen cold as sparks in Plato's Cave,
each of us intent on a reel of shadows
flickering like television in our heads,
while he'd have trooped us through a world
of Forms, which was what he loved best,
the soul's furnishings arranged in perfect
rooms of thought,

each attribute without flaw—
like the whitewashed walls of this parlor
hung with the owner's family portraits
grown forlorn in his absence, as though
lifted from their fixtures they floated
through space, no longer here, like us
watched by what's foreign,
as we imagine ourselves at home—
this sofa our couch, these knickknacks
shipped to somewhere else, shelves

filled with books, and each studied room
a dream of forgotten life.

Our realtor takes such care,
pointing out cracks in plaster, slippages
of kitchen tiles, floorboards, runs his eye
across walls, ceilings, checks the basement
circuit box, wanting, it seems, what's best
for us, inspecting the house as if it were
an argument of the world's soundness,
in every niche a subtlety. And we follow
like disciples who want to believe
Here is where we belong, sunlight
burnishing the windowpanes, the dust
hazed and swirling like first stars.

Miranda

From my window I watch the flurries whirl
Milan into dream, and clothe the duomo's dome
in robes of sheerest gauze. Each day the faithful
haul more marble to the masons, sculptors,
busy at their arts. Turrets, spires rise
beside brave saints, gargoyles—so elaborately slow,
like a masque whose movements bore us to belief.
My father's down below, all thoughts dead, blind
to this prospering. They say it will take centuries.
He sleeps between a bishop and a Medici.

I never knew why he named me for wonder;
or was it my mother. No matter—
in the backward of time, he's nearly all I knew.
To this day, however hard I try, I remember
nothing of my life before exile, only vague shapes
of handmaids in gowns, indistinguishable
as statues in this snow, indistinguishable
as those doting on me now. I do not know
my mother's face. It's as if memory itself
were my father's shifting island, full of noises;
though however hard I listen, her spirit's voice
is one I never hear. But I hear his still,
turbulent as the storms he'd conjure at a whim,
or justify by some auspicious star.

For hours he'd linger in his cell
that was dank and claustral as a monk's hut
poring over books, talking to himself,
or summoning powers I could not see
while I spied darkly through a wall of reeds.
Intonations. Biddings. Gibberish. His lips
moved like the tremblings of a bird,
so different from when he'd speak to me.
So, when he cloistered himself,

that's when I'd feel most free
pretending to have run of the island.
These were my spirits: hidden springs gushed
from the forest floor, moss-slicked stones,
swollen lagoons, the hush of palms
in quickening winds, huge fronds that drooped
sullenly and smelled of skunk, sweet pulp
of outsized fruits, tidal hiss; the poked eye
of a jellyfish in the foam, dolphin plash
in a glitter of waves. And best of all,
the tulips, dark-hearted and voluptuous,
that I'd linger over, almost tasting
their color on my tongue.

Sometimes in those times alone
I'd lie among dunes and dream an island
full of people; or muse myself a strong god
with power to sink the sea beneath the land.
To think of it after so many years, I see now
how near I was to the first child
of those shores. Was he really so very ugly?
That night, when he came to my bed, misshapen
thing, and spoke to me, and put his hand
over my mouth, I could hear my father's voice
in his consuming eloquence, and the same
mastering need to control.

Little joy after that, till the storm,
till Ferdinand, bestowed from the sea.
How could I not be drawn to him, for twelve years
having known no one but those two, no one
of my sex? I liked his body, liked his laugh,
though he wanted as lover, always troubled
by affairs of court. Still, he had a tenderness.
Awkward prince, my king, that's what I clung to

years after the vow diminished to chess games
at night in the parlor. Sometimes, I wish
we had stayed on the island, spurned the contract,
the promises of state, spurned my father's wish.
I remember how they spoke that day, past and future
aside, like conspirators, plotting my life,
as if I were nothing more than my father's gift.
Milan, the island, Naples, again Milan…
I'm tired of the tricks of dukes and kings,
how always they turn to the audience for approval,
childish ploy to make them feel they're loved.
My father's dead these forty years, my husband nearly ten,
who together made me queen. Let the others fade,
all courts and counselors, gaggles of men preening
in costume. But I'll remember Caliban,
who like me lost a mother to the arts of men.
How often I think I see his shape in the shape
of this cathedral's carved stone—creature, whose voice
is rain and wind, grimacing under its weight.

The Hunt-Cup

It's a long time since the dawn chase over shires,
hoof-beats gathering in the half-light, human wails
and the dog-pack barking in earnest, surging
for the flash through gorse, the prey manic for its lair,

leaping over tree-roots, rifling through thickets,
desperate as the fugitive whose fear encodes the wind.
Now the escaped slave can rest on his long journey north,
the scars of chains, whippings healed to infant's skin;

now the last Jew left in the ghetto, a pack
of storm-troopers trained on his shivering body,
can stand in the open singing his lost ones home;
and the children of Kurdistan, El Mozote,

of Armenia, Capetown, Kigali, Sarajevo,
of all the cities of unremembered death,
have rewound the black scrolls of their intestines
and are dancing in the squares in a joy before language.

It's an Indian summer evening in New Hope.
And our host has served us sherry in a hunt-cup,
its sterling stem, a fox's head sniffing the air
like Anubis reared in judgment over the dead

who would drink of the waters of forgetfulness:
a sweet bouquet and perfect finish. Nowhere do men
bend over their riven trophy, draining its life,
partaking of this chalice as if it housed a god;

nowhere has the wind stopped dead in its tracks,
like a mother in the aftermath of massacre
refusing the offered cup, the whole world
distilled into a thimbleful of blood.

Deep Shit

I can't remember the name of the gaunt monk
who stroked my face during confession
years ago in that bare abbey room,
Tell me what's wrong, son, tell me what's wrong,
his fingers soft as a grandmother's, his eyes
deep and pleading; nor can I remember
what I told him—something about the pain
of feeling alone, something grim and adolescent—
my back arched against the wall. *Deep shit,*
I said to myself, *You're in deep shit,*
though his hand didn't travel any further,
and I confessed my sins, forgave the indiscretion.
Afterwards, I walked out along a road
puddled by afternoon rain as I whispered the prayer
of the lost—something facile and earnest,
something parroted and true: *Show me the way*.
Before I knew (who could make this up?),
I was ankle-deep in cow dung, deep shit,
my life already steeped in allegory:
Christian hunkered in the Slough of Despond,
Everyman forsaken by all but Good Deeds.
Though now it's *Midnight Cowboy* I think of,
how Joe Buck discovers he'll do anything
to keep alive—turn tricks in dank theaters,
bash an old man's face with a phone to save
Ratso his friend, who dies anyway.
I'm lonely, lonely the crazed queen howls,
root of all evil, before he presses our hero
to kneel and Joe, pure of heart, breaks free
into the sleazy New York night, his journey
to the promised land of Florida begun
in the waste he's made of his life, his deep shit:
deep shit, or whatever it is, even mishandled,
that draws us somehow beyond ourselves—
what moved the old priest to stroke my face,

his need to touch, to be touched, more powerful
than any vow. Yes, it's lonely, lonely,
like the nameless crosses of the abbey graves
where the monks perform their final wordless prayer,
O deep shit to be sure—something broken
and unbearable, something ineluctable and long.

Homage to Bartolomé de Las Casas

In this century, and moment, of mania
Tell me a story.
Make it a story of great distances…
Robert Penn Warren, *Audubon: A Vision*

Proem: The Narrows

For here between two worlds, another, harsh,
This third, of water, tests the word…
Hart Crane, *The Bridge*

From our roof in Brooklyn, I could see the Narrows
through an alley between rowhouses, and ships
churning beyond Shore Road into Gravesend
and, farther, beyond Sandy Hook into the Atlantic.

Even at night, in fog, the lights of the Verrazzano,
like a necklace hung on nothing, shimmered.
Freighters, tankers, sounded through absence
and, sometimes, Visitation's bells would ring in answer.

Home was the only story told to me. I'd climb
over the seawall at low tide to squat on rocks
slick with moss, and palm the water. And the river
touched me back, though I knew only one of its names.

I. The Admiral Returns

In 1493, at the age of 18, Bartolomé de las Casas, son of a Spanish businessman, witnessed Columbus's triumphant return from the new world when "The Admiral of the Ocean Seas" paraded through the streets of Seville with seven Taino Indians, exotic parrots, and other spoils of his journey…

In that time so new and like no other
the sum of what we are exceeds the known.
On hill and river, the Spanish sun burns,
while throughout the town bells speak in tongues
and crowds swarm before the Arch of Images
to capture a glimpse of the miracle

parading through the square. "It's a miracle
they've come back at all," someone says. Others,
concentrating on the Arch, its images

of glories past, begin to stir with the unknown.
Beggar, soldier, tradesman, don—rumors burn
along the air until, at once, all tongues

cry out to greet the pageant, as if the tongues
of angels rose exultant at some miracle:
"*Christum Ferens*," "new settler," his name burned
flagrant in the book of fame. Mothers
lift children to witness things to make the known
pale, shudder before the rush of images:

seven natives, sporting feathers, each the image
of a wild bird, and birds behind, their tongues
clacking each to each like those natives who know
no one, huddling to themselves, chained miracles
painted bright as stained glass, alike as brothers
beneath flapping banners as curiosity burns

like temptation in the soul's continent, burns
like an inquisitor's pyre—as if the scrimmage
with "Hell" were won, Jews banished, the other
infidels routed; heretics plied with tongs
to mark the one true path in this miracle
year given to God and conquest. He will own

the like of these, the young man in the crowd, known
for his family, his good breeding. As on an urn
the animal's brought to sacrifice, a miracle
of nature, though not created in the image
of God, so these seven born of a different tongue—
barbarians—march where no one asks another

"Is this all that can be known of miracles,
a god's twisted image cast in gold, the tongue
ripped burning from the mouth of the other?"

II. New World

Scent of sweetgum rising
from night fires, dawn
lacing the palms, cedars
wide as oxen, the moon
a pale shield dissolving
in the west. This morning,
awash in mist, the *cay*
could be a caravel
and the young man who wakes
to his chosen vistas
the watchman who spotted
the providential flock.
Below his villa, *bohíos*
stir with families,
gentle sheep entrusted
by God to our care,
now assembled, now marched
inland along paths
glutted with cassava,
canopied with grapes.
To him the future's
a navigable sea,
branch plucked from the tides,
covered with dogroses—
a prophecy, a sign.
Out of sight: the rivers,
children hunching for gold;
out of sight: the mines,
baskets of hands
buzzing with flies…

In 1502, Bartolomé himself sailed for the Indies and lived for many years like the other colonists, holding slaves on his encomienda, *or plantation, in Hispaniola (called Arimao), steadily improving his lot with the colonial governors despite taking vows as a chaplain…*

III. A Baptism

It was not until 1514, sometime after witnessing the massacre at Caonao, Cuba, during the Pacification, that Fra Bartolomé eschewed "the savage writ" of the encomienda *system...*

Always when we entered a province
it was the same, the people plentiful
as the wild grapes above our heads,
a hundred loads within the circle
of a crossbow's shot;
                                        and me, banding
the children together to be baptized
while the soldiers pursued their customs,
not content with what was freely given,
but raiding stores, raping wives and daughters.
The natives honored me for the comforts
I'd give,
                till I became in their eyes
like their own magicians, priests, healers,
and they'd do reverence, knowing I meant no harm.
That morning, outside Caonao, our troop
breakfasted in a riverbed, only a few
small pools where the sky reflected
like torn pieces of a robe. It was full
of whetstones, and the men desired

to sharpen their swords on them.
Thousands greeted us in the town square,
some bringing gifts—cassava bread and fish,
gourds filled with water—others squatting
as is their custom, staring, frightened
at our mares. One of the mounted soldiers
drew his sword, and in a heartbeat
a hundred followed.
                                        Then, O precious Christ,
they began to rip the bellies of those lambs.
Within two credos no one remained alive,
no one in the square. Not satisfied,

soldiers flooded the groves, the *bohíos*,
as I ran everywhere to stop the killing,
cursing the insolent captain's boast—
"How does Your Honor like what we have done?"

Of all those dead, one haunts me still,
that young man no older than our Lord
who wept as he bled his guts into my hands.
"If I baptize you, you will go to live with God"
I told him, and through his anguish he said yes.
To his blood and the rest, in Christ's, I give witness.

IV. Interlude: A Reverse Fish

(Remora eel, Cuba, 1514)

Threaded through tail-fin
as through a needle's eye,
the line pays out fathoms,
trailing the mouth
through shallows to its haunt
inside the turtle's shell,
the gaping O a hook
sucking sustenance
from its bulk till both
are drawn back, instinct
plotted to technology,
the man's hand prying
the shell free of its meat,
the used tool broken
to pieces in the sand.

V. First Conversion
(Espíritu Santo, Hispaniola – Pentecost, 1514)

...through which so
many natives lost
their lives, gave up
his wealth, and began
to preach against the
system. Called a heretic
for refusing to grant
penance to those holding
slaves; called also a
lunatic and a traitor...

That morning when he pushed away from shore
in the small canoe paddled by natives,
did a light leap up from the calm of the river

calling his name? So, he fell backwards
into verse from Ecclesiastes
and a reverie of broken promises—

Like the man who murders his brother
is the thief who offers sacrifice
from the possessions of the poor.

Or was it a sudden sting of fear, the sight
of his own death cruising through the brush,
whispered in the murmur of leaves, till one night

it strikes, reducing the spirit to ash?
Or maybe it was the allegory
his life was becoming, increase of a wish

that forced itself to this crux, this now
that ghosted him since home. Far-flung, fortyish,
he steadies himself in the boat's hollow,

dabbles his hand in the current, a rush
of arrows moving through reflected sky,
each scrap of shore piloted in the hush.

He might be the young man who questioned Christ,
How can I be saved? And the savior
told him what he already knew, what this priest

knew the thousand times he'd read the words,
Give up everything you have, their light
finally clarified in his casting off.

Downstream, the congregation gathers
for the pliant sermon, the savage writ
sanctioned to which he'll put the sword.

Already angry faces in the flux
cry out their condemnations—*madman, heretic*—
as the quick oars lift and pierce the river's flesh.

VI. Utopias
(Venezuela, 1521)

...for fifty years Las Casas fought for native rights, traveling throughout the Indies and South America, attempting unsuccessfully to establish utopian communities where natives would share in the profits of their labors...

All things are possible
in Christ, even this: to build
the New Jerusalem here, where rainforest
shields from sight the bones of tortured slaves,
abundant harvest

of the predestined,
the remnant swarming to the father's blessing
who would arrive like an unexpected god
with big plans, best intentions, the masters
trembling at his word.

Cumaná, Teziutlán—
each name to be christened,
each city planned in the image of the One
around whom the turning world revolves,
till nothing's random,

    the years plotted over
  to just apportions of work and prayer,
and brute and victim live together in true peace.
    This is nowhere, the good man's
      wish laid waste

    by what? by pride?
  by the system? by the judgment of his God?
Let his soul be a boat stranded in dead calm,
    the captain incompetent, his hands to heaven,
      waiting for wind.

VII. A Volcano
(Inferno de Marsaya, 1536)

Above the white-hot core the pure sky burns,
A cloud-range back-lit in sulfur and gold.
What truth endures beneath the flaming stream?

In seething ships, the Africans come in streams
Like Christ to take the place of those who burn—
The flayed, native skin that is the conqueror's gold

The priest hoped to save, for love of God not gold,
Though blood runs through time like a molten stream.
He watches from his perch the earth's offing burn

Gold, black, and red. This world's the burning stream.

VIII. Protector of the Indians
(Arrival in Chiapas, 1544)

...advocating the Indian case in court and in his writings, serving for a time as bishop of Chiapas in southern Mexico...

Those lulls were the spirit's stagnant seas
we left behind with our lost,
nine priests shipwrecked, my library
scattered to mucky shoals; behind us,
half the Spanish court praying
for my death.

So that morning
when we finally came ashore,
seeing my own people's turned backs,
hearing their curses, their obscene songs,
I steeled myself with *canciones*
sung to men bloodied as newborns,
draped in the flayed skins of their gods.
How ardently they listened, like children
spellbound by fables whose good news
would waken them from sleep.

We told them of our first parents,
their fall, of a Father's love
great enough to sacrifice his only Son
so that everyone might be saved,
if only they believed. And they did:
friars baptizing them in jungle streams,
some taking vows, proof
the soul knows its true home
no matter the distances of flesh.

Even their rites, savage, the chosen
splayed alive on altars:
all raw promises of our hope.
As though truth lay buried like a seed

in earth, our coming to these lands
a gracious rain to quicken the Lord's
improbable fruit.

But these unregenerate
of my own barbarous race
who turn their backs on their God
and fashion idols of gold,
making property of their fellowmen
whom they crush like dung in the streets,
who can fathom so rank a refusal?

In my sermons I tell them this,
and pray for their redemption.
Each moment, had we eyes to see,
Christ stands before us, His body
a veil parted open, beckoning;
holding in His hand a beacon—
His own living heart torn free.

IX. Sepúlveda
(Valladolid, 1550)

Who can deny gunpowder against pagans
is the burning of incense to Our Lord?
That morning, spoiled for the Great Debate,
I was the sword's edge of reason
to steel any cardinal's bleeding heart
against his womanlier sentiments,
upholding the perfect logic of the faith—
Christ triumphant, Christ over all.

Day-long I dispensed my syllogisms
like fine pearls before the gallery,

...and in 1550 debating the humanist Juan Ginés de Sepúlveda who held that natives were "slaves by nature" and therefore justifiably subdued. Because of Las Casas's defense, the Church refused to grant its imprimatur to Sepúlveda's work, and new, more temperate laws were established to govern Spanish colonies...

sensing whispered assents in the hush,
and sealed my case with Aristotle:
As the body to the soul, beasts to men,
so, by nature, are slaves to their masters.
What more could I have done to prove us just
save flaunting a brute bloodied with sacrifice?

Later, when the old priest entered the hall
to offer his refutation, his face
had the unshakable look of a prophet
slightly mad. Five days he droned stories
of brutes brutalized, of brutes our equal
in the image of God—as though apes
commanded reason—and us a river
of molten flame savaging those lands.

Who'd have thought the judges could be swayed
to tolerate such folly, though I'm certain
his tack was to wear them down. You
who will witness us from a later time
note this: Las Casas was a hypocrite,
loving the distant image of himself
in native eyes till they called him father.
But I will have history's imprimatur.

X. Second Conversion
(San Gregorio Monastery, Valladolid, 1555)

Bartolomé de las Casas, popularly called "Protector of the Indians," died in 1566 in Atocha Monastery in Madrid, after having written the first bill of human rights in the New World…

So, this is the voice
of God, the heartless
charge casting
you down
like a pearl diver
into deep, that sound

you swim through
naked, your eyes
marking fathoms
for sharks,
for the slick
treasure you pray
is there, years
of this, your hands
un-coding the bottom,
the little net you carry
permeable
as hope, your hair
grown ashen as
a prophet's,
your skin a seal's,
till one day you
emerge and
there it is: the jeweled
irritant, the perfect
pearl—

We must give back
everything.

Coda: Last Rites
(Atocha Monastery, Madrid, 1566)

He maintained at the end of his life that for their cruelties the colonists should be banished from their settlements so that the remaining natives may restore themselves "to their human and temporal good way of life."

A boy's perched in a tree, his hair
plaited with straw, in his free hand
a parrot he taps lightly once
on his florid crest, and it cries out
like someone driven by the sword.
Now countless parrots come, hearing
the captive, and the boy reaches
with his slender stick, a thin cord

at the end looping the birds' necks,
which he wrings, dropping them below.

The dream ends, drifts to the next
without regard, without passion
that would transform the boy into God
luring us painfully to Himself;
into history, its feathered meat
piled in millions under the tree.
Hoods hover in the claustral cell
above the wracked face of Las Casas,
the chrism a glistening film
like palm oil on his forehead,

his fingers ink-stained with tomes
written *for God alone and from*
compassion at seeing perish
such multitudes of rational men.
Fifty years—even in canoes
a cloister of books borne in crates
to Chiapas, to Verapaz…
Now the hand holds out its candle,
I have done so little, a speck
of sun harboring in the dark.

From *The Narrows* (2005)

The metaphysical desire does not long to return, for it is desire for a land not of our birth, for a land foreign to every nature which has not been the land of our parents, and to which we shall never betake ourselves.

Emmanuel Levinas, *Totality and Infinity*

And Máel Dúin said: "Leave the boat in rest without rowing and wherever it shall please God to bring, he will bring [it]." Then they entered the great, limitless ocean…

The Voyage of Máel Dúin

Proem: Double Life

The Sky Road

To have been born on the very edge of things
in a whitewashed hut with blonde bangs of thatch
and an unlatched gate that leads into the open,
sky and sky beyond the window onto land's end,
everything blending and the ocean shattered with light

and not to be this strange face peering through a hedge
your dead once walked beside, earrings of fuchsia
astride the rock wall: it is no nostalgia
but the plain air of things, the very curb of exile,
this dwelling on the edge where you are born.

Headlands

To have driven along blue levitating roads
this far into land's end, golden, rumpled,
these humps that could be the goddess's bedclothes,
and that red broach of a bridge pinning the continent
together; it is all ample and errant

like this wind and the garrulous ocean below
bellowing on in the voice of Whitman
Death, death, death, death, death on the wrong shore,
the horizon as much behind us as before,
always our eyes rising to the sky's imprint on tar.

from The Narrows

The similitudes of the past and those of the future…
Walt Whitman, "Crossing Brooklyn Ferry"
For Nora Ruane, ni Hughes

I. *Mural*

The way Lanning painted it, Benton, Rivera—bright panels
on which the laborers huddle, shirtless, their flexed arms
bearing the full weight of the rail.
Representative men,
without names but for Paddy, Dago, Gook,
so the foreman calls them, shotgun slung behind his back
as he rides towards the Iron Horse somewhere deep
in the continent:
Death Valley and Donner Pass,
rock-faces sheer, indifferent—
or patient, as if to say *This rabble won't last long.*

To the left: natives lounge on empty prairie, wagons,
homesteaders tying bales of hay,
a horse-drawn thresher.
To the right: turbines
squat as bombs, stokers at a furnace, a mother and infant
climbing into their crowded cart that will disappear
down the cavern walls of the street. A woman
leans out her window in a posture of regret.
Someone leaving,
someone not coming back,
while dead center of the mural others hammer the ties—

Lives scaled out of lives along the panorama's strict expanse…

~

My father drives the gaudy pink Rambler
down Bay Ridge Avenue to the Shore,
the great wooden pier jutting into the Narrows—flood-tide,
bright flow—where the ferry luffs against its moorings,

its wide iron ramp laid down for the line of cars that slow,
then roll snugly into its belly,
                                        me in back between my mother
and her mother, Nora, who carries herself regally
as the Guggenheims whose children she nannied
when she first came over.
                                        Quayside at Cobh,
under St. Colman's spire, she waited at the pier,
black Mayo dirt smoored into her shoes,
daughter of a remnant, of *clachan* and *rundale*,
cottier and *meithall*, the big ships made imaginable
on postcards distributed at crossroads in the townlands,
on signs posted in market villages: Dominion,
Cunard, White Star Line—"Splendid Accommodation"
for the exile, for the *deori*:

"There's nothing for you here."

~

The tender putters to its floating palace,
in the distance, Spike Island, Davitt's Rock.
For days in steerage, she's one of the thousand
packed inside, the bunks camp-hung and numbered,
the boat heaving
                              to the Atlantic, as though each roll
were prelude to an undertow.
It's nearly a week before she comes to the rail,
the ship steaming past Sandy Hook, the Moriches,
the Narrows a *causey*
                                  "of a highway where sky
comes down to water." There the Statue stands,
torch in hand
                            above the dumbstruck hordes,
above the gleaming cityscape, *caisleán óir*,

castles of gold, mythic as Tír na nÓg.
She's alone
as she queues off the gangway for the Great Hall
with its iron bars, an assembly line
of stations and pens, its marble alive with tongues.

It is as if the *throughother* of her familiar fields
had changed in a dream she only now awakens to,
the manifest tag pinned to her lapel,
a gripped inspection card, barked commands
from the uniform at the gate, from the uniform on the stairs.
She stiffens as she's handled, so many hands, her eyelids
twisted back with a buttonhook, the man ahead marked
with chalk, a brusque X on his coat
before he's shuffled away.
What's your name? Where are you going? What's your trade?
Have you a job? Can you read this?

—"Let my sentence come forth from thy presence;
Let thine eyes behold the things that are equal."—

Then the shower, a baptism, the old world washed free.

And she's through,
the Island behind her with its dormitories and detainees,
caged yard and infirmary, walls glyphic with names,
the ferry bearing her to open road—fifty years:
a husband, five children, a first son outlived…

~

Her Brooklyn of ample hills rises behind us,
bricked-up, paved over
as our ferry pushes into the Narrows
for our trip west. Ahead: Todt Hill, the terminal

at St. George.
Skyscrapers crowd to the brink
of the Battery.
And as the boat loafs into the harbor—
a panorama of docks,
liners lumbering out to sea, tugs and tankers
where the bare steel towers of the bridge soar, half-risen,
over Gravesend,
the Hudson pouring itself along the Palisades,
the Statue a green flame in the middle of it all.
And already
my grandmother is out of the car for a better view,
shoring her new hat against the wind.

II. *Archive*

The rules are strict inside the archive—no food, no bags,
no talking beyond this point.
And don't forget
to take a number, line up for instruction
from the stern administrator, who, it turns out,
is politer than he looks, directing me patiently
in how to use the volumes of categories and codes,
as if these tomes were history's phone books,
as if each of us could dial our origins.

Registries, ships' lists, census reports, the boxes
and their corresponding dates
piled ceiling-high along the aisles
in the light's fluorescent haze.
The archive is a Chinese box, a maze
that draws me further in, each filmed list
a laboratory slide of DNA—

Nora Ruane, ni Hughes,
of Kilvindoney. Her stone in Calvary
reads 1900, though she lied about her age, recited
the rosary in her small kitchen afternoons
when I came home from school,

—"Get me a cruller, Danny, from Sally's,
and yourself a hamburger and I'll make tea…"—

For as long as I knew her, she lived apart
from my grandfather, Martin, immobile
in a nursing home, our visits
become flickers in an unlit room.
Though my mother kept his passport—
British Subject, 1918, aged twenty years—
in the hope chest with her keepsakes.

In a gray, dated box I find the likely reels.
Whir of machines
in the viewing room, tapes unspooling microscopic lists,
bright squares like the subway's lit-up windows
across the black bar of film.
The cards, hastily typed,
run in spate down the screen where I sit, scanning
the sounds of names, until, finally, I read
Martin Ruane, arrived April 8th, 1920,
S.S. Kaiserin Auguste Victoria.
But how did he travel from Ballyhaunis
to Liverpool, the Prince's Dock, where the Irish were thick,
as Hawthorne wrote, "like maggots in cheese"?

And where did they meet, born
twenty miles apart, in different townlands?
Not in the port, not in Claremorris.
For her name I need to scroll further back—

Harlan, Hellas, Hugo, Hughes:
ten Nora Hughes's—earliest 1910, most likely 1915—
arrived on *The Celtic* to New York out of Cobh.

Did they love each other?

I'd heard of marriages arranged, families
gathered by county in their new neighborhoods.
In the photo she kept on her bedroom dresser
they looked so properly posed.

I remember how she grieved when he died,
keening her first son's name with her husband's
in the funeral parlor's smoky hall…

III. *West*

To begin, love: our fingers on the map's crimped horizon,
following roads that run inland from the sea,
tracing the way west
in the clear light of our rented room—
Lucan, Clonard, Horseleap, Athlone, the names
reeling off
lyrics sung to their own accompaniment,
all the way to Ballinrobe.
Outside, the teeming puzzle
of Dublin streets converges at the Liffey,
then out along the quays toward Kilmainham, Chapelizod.

It's all out of scale,
this naming and the thing named, as though the map
were territory,
and yet such frisson brings lift-off,
like the giddiness of our flight

above the Narrows, the city receding behind us, the bridge
grown small as a safety pin, clipping the islands
as we banked along the coast, leaving
the continent behind,
                                        only a few boats below,
fish glistening into the ocean's huge nothing.

~

Who cares if it's all fiction, this romance of origins,
a farmhouse in a townland outside Ballinrobe,
stories rehearsed a hundred times
                                        across a kitchen table?
How my grandmother had to leave, like her sisters
but one, Winnie, the youngest, turned back from Ellis Island,
a chalk "E" scratched on her coat, her eyes
already glazing under the buttonhook
into those two moons,
                                        and her stooped
as though searching for something lost.

Or how Tommy, her brother, ruled the house,
and would not let her visit family in America—
dollar bills pinned on walls beside holy pictures,
a brother and sister, like an old couple,
bent in silence before the hearth.

~

Here, driving free of town, the rotaries
run clockwise, the roadway
a mirror image of our familiar path.

My grandfather might have traveled east
along a version of this route

to one of the channel boats moored along the Liffey.
"Scholar," his passport read.
                    Did he leave for the "better life,"
like the millions who left because they had to go?

From Brize to Ballyhaunis, all the way to Eden Quay,
he followed the path of the long meadow,
as though to join that earlier train,
those who'd starved in their sod hovels,
                                        the sod itself
a last meal caking in their mouths.

And there was my grandfather, Martin, like Nora,
leaving by cart or train—who knows how?—
a generation later, finding their place
                                      in the prospect
of a canvas too vast to envision whole.

~

Is that what it means to be an American,
discovering yourself in the distances?—

                   Like a man on a Greyhound
that leaves the New York Port Authority
and takes the Lincoln Tunnel to the Interstate.
It's after dark, all the man can see are headlights
                      passing, a blur of malls and subdivisions.
He sleeps in his seat beside a stranger,
                               wakes when the bus pulls in
to a late-night road stop. He's not hungry,
but feels in his gut a tremor
                                  of loneliness that grows
as they pass through Ohio, Indiana,
the furnaces of Hammond and Gary,

fierce as Blake's Satanic mills,
spewing into the boundless prairie sky.
He looks out for a thousand miles
at the hypnotic emptiness of wheat fields and cornfields,
the cinematic grandeur of the Rockies,
and descends from the Wasatch
to the Great Salt Lake,
a sunset spreading over the earth...

What he wants
is to stand at the other end of it all, to see
the Pacific rolling into headlands
like visible waves of light,
and then to turn back,
the bridge stretching out over the bay below him,
another Narrows,
until he sees that there is no end,
just these waves of water waves of land
flung together,
feeling on his face the rush of wind,
and inside him the growing thought that anywhere
might be home,
since home has become nowhere.

~

It is like our standing present now
before this ancestral house
passed to unfamiliar hands,
its thatch removed years ago, a modern extension
jutting out back from whitewashed clay walls.
No one home.
And as we peer through the window,
the hearth inscribes its arc
halfway up the wall, its border painted brightly,

an old-time kettle at the center—
                                                    Winnie dead, Tommy dead,
a line of unknown faces trailing back,
                                              fanning forward,
our own to be among them,
as if now were the space between facing mirrors,
life's after-life of lives indwelling.

And already it's renewing itself,
the memory of our car ride across a country
                                                  that is not our own,
checking the map, stopping to find our bearings,
our lunch in a town called Gortaleam,
how we bickered about the right road,
but made our way—
                                      the church at the crossroads
in Robeen, the cemetery in the field
                          where Winnie and Tommy are buried
with their parents, Sabena and Martin,
all the names on a single stone—
                                                     then, so close,
losing our way again, stopping to ask directions
to Kilvindoney—its four farmhouses on stony ground
twenty miles from the Atlantic,
              how the old farmer leaned his windblown face
to our window before pointing us the way:

                              —"Is it Hughes you're wanting?
                                  O, they're all gone."

Pallbearers at Emily Dickinson's Funeral

Death but the Drift of Eastern Gray,
Dissolving into Dawn away,
Before the West begin –
Emily Dickinson

She died at sunset facing west,
her own society
his room—her soul—its offing
a vastness like the sea

these six endured on coffin ships,
her bark their burden now,
in her hands two heliotropes
whose mind was measured noon.

Each Consciousness must emigrate.
Her passage stayed at home,
while these stalwarts made literal
the crux of their *immram*

through swells of gray immensity,
their terms in remnant holds,
and wakes distilled their ecstasies
until they fathomed here.

Now horizon is this transit
admitted by the train
that passes through her rose estates
into unstopped expanse.

They bear her single privacy
surpassed, as coal to pearl—
the center and circumference
cracked open like a seal.

The meadow opens through the gate,
a Paradise of Now,
where cricket consorts play the bones
above the undertow.

Incense of apple blossom drifts
with bell notes in the trees—
and resurrection's skiffs embark
at dew's velocity.

Aftermath

9/11/01

It will not be
how the saint imagined,

the soul distilling
into what comes after

the way a woman
wades into ocean

that laps her skin
at body temperature

so she feels herself
the waves' completion,

a fluency
of wine in water,

her body all flow
as she slides under

then out of herself
like a silk nightgown

though you wish it so,
though you wish it so.

Instead, these ashes
through the flood-lit night,

through the silent heaven,
rising, rising…

A Mosque in Brooklyn

There is no prayer that can abolish history,
though in this basement mosque the muezzin's history

gathers in his throat like a tenor's aria
and he calls to God to put an end to history.

From my courtyard room I hear his song ascending,
the divine name whirling its rebuke to history—

Allah, Allah—above the crowded rowhouse roofs.
Their rusted antennas, stalled arrows of history,

would transmit a daily riot of talk and news,
the world boxed inside a glowing square of history.

I've seen them on the street, the faithful in their robes
walking along store-fronts, a different history

clothing them, like me, in our separate skins,
though here we are at the scope-end of history:

Goodness is timeless, the great English poet wrote,
and not just for himself—the crime is history.

But as if to prove the old Sufi fable true
these prayers are lifted on the thermals of history,

and sound strangely like that congregation of birds—
no, the remnant who survived a blighted history,

having stayed their quest into the final valley
where a Great Tree rose, its branches thick as history.

And there they lost themselves, flourishing into the One
without division, without names, without history.

At the Tree of Many, One

I.

Behind our house in Grossi's single field,
  the sun slides below cedars,
    sky tilted to dusk.
    All day I've played
    in junkyard, shale-pit,
  darted through woods with a plastic rifle,
  till now, waist-deep in blowing grass,
I stop shock-still at the sound of my name—
At this moment you might have fled us,
    called back from our games
    at the snub-end of summer,
or driven like a catkin through the quickening air.

II.

    Who called me back
    was not my mother,
    who lay in her bed
in the hospital overlooking the Narrows
where she heard the doctor's words
"She came too soon, we couldn't save her..."
Outside her window: bridge-lights
    suspended in fog,
a string of pearls her nurse said.
So years later my mother confessed to me,
her voice thin as thread through a needle's eye.

III.

  Colleen Regina. Kathleen Ann.
Names bestowed on wished-for lives...

Those late nights in our kitchen,
my father asleep, my brother gone
from that house's angers,
I listened as she nursed
another drink to stories
of dolls and shopping, braided hair,
a daughter close as a sister—
the ideal world she created
in a haze of regrets, how always
a mother loses her sons.
In those hours you became a thought
almost palpable, a hint of smoke
drifted from her cigarette,
or a soul's spark poised for release.

IV.

Once, an ancient hymn recounts, a child
travels from his father's house
to rescue a single pearl
guarded by a serpent in the sea.
Putting off his robe of glory, the boy
descends into Egypt,
and as happens in such stories,
forgets the purpose of his quest,
seduced by customs of an alien land—
though like clockwork comes the awakening:
the pearl saved, his inheritance restored.
But why does the child leave at all?
And what's the worth of a pearl
for a house so surfeited with wealth?
So we renounce the myth, turn from it
the way tourists turn
from beggars; say meaning moves

from life to life without a trace,
so when we come to the end it is this truth
we see: the serpent
coiled around a black hole.
And you who never left, who have no need
of stories, what knowledge
can you give us who pause
on the journey outward
only to feel inside the drag of created things?

V.

In the beginning: an atom of time,
atom of space, flung gasses,
I see you, sister,
lured back in return—
fetus, fish, single-cell, nil.
There, in those final waters,
you are again
what we can no longer be:
uncreated, an absence
from which even God's hand emerges.

VI.

The Time Capsule
on our bookshelf
took up two shelves.
Each night I'd pick a year
to pore over pictures
of a century's events.
This was history,
quickened by a whiff of mildew:

Kitty Hawk rising
over Carolina dunes, depression
breadlines, trenches at Verdun,
an era's assorted portraits;
on the couch our father
watching television, who survived
Guam, Leyte Gulf, the pier
explosion at Luckenbach
where he woke with his friend lying
dead on top of him
the year before I was born,
the dock's air
thick with voices of the dead
summoning their one prayer of reversal,
the way the Narrows' surf
seethes in its breakers:
what if, what if, what if, what if…
What pursues me? Everything
you've missed.

VII.

That I am, that I am—there's no sorrow
greater, the contemplative said,
than to feel this "naked spark of being":
and so he leaves his name
to our unknowing. Yet this self-taste,
how vividly it stung the poet
until he saw in everything—
windhover, ploughman, poplar, wreck—
the charge of mastering grandeur.
Height and length and breadth,
all that gives shape to this earth,
must be put behind a cloud, must be

forgotten, with every creature,
for you will not be perfect in love
until this too is destroyed.
To what purpose then do we long
to preserve the illusion,
this real earth, we who are not like you,
who would make our lives
leaves pressed deeply into a book
that cures and keeps and heals our memory?

VIII.

Sister, those stone walls, overrun by ferns,
that divided each field, come back to me.
And the Narrows, its freighters sounding
through thickest fog. This world
calls like a neighbor through the dusk.
Again, the wind steps over your soul.

from Pearl Court

To inhabit oneirically the house we were born in means
more than to inhabit it in memory; it means living in this house
that is gone, the way we used to dream in it…
Gaston Bachelard, *The Poetics of Space*

My Grandmother's Apartment

A slow air's modulated hush
gathers to jig and reel—
John Gibbons' pressed accordion
propped on his wooden leg,
his face puffed fat as a peony
above his buttoned mustard collar
and green serge coat,
his eyes flagrantly bright.
Whenever he'd arrive
I'd follow him from the foyer,
rapt with his hampered walk,
then sit at his feet staring
at the false limb in disbelief
while the rest of the family
kept time around the table,
their feet tapping out rhythms
on scuffed linoleum.
Clachan music. Riffs of her past
my mother's mother carried over
from the lost hearth. Each day,
home after school, I'd make
my visitation, sit with her
in the darkened kitchen
as her fingers clicked
through her rosary, her lips
tremulous with prayer.
Then, awash in the ritual,
I'd fetch us crullers
from Sally's Luncheonette
as she put on the kettle.
On her bedroom dresser she kept

a ceramic bust of Christ
with his right hand pointing
to the crown of his sacred heart
and its ring of flames, a secret
compartment in back that held
holy water and chrism,
her plain wooden crucifix
with its soldered Jesus,
she'd say, for when He takes me.
Now I come back to this house,
with nostalgia for tea and sweets
shared in dimly lit rooms,
for a promise of life eternal
sculpted in tacky shrines,
to praise one-legged men
with squeeze boxes
that open and close like fans,
or like a blacksmith's bellows
to raise from the emptiness song.

Bridge View

The grandeur of the tower was nothing at first
but our surmise at what it would become,
gleaned from rumors; though before long
we watched the stanchions' gradual ascent
above Shore Road's distant stand of trees
where Third narrowed to its vanishing point.

Nothing at first, and then, from the corner,
one day we saw the legs barely risen,
two sheer columns of iron and steel:
the tensile thighs of a man being built
foot by lifted foot from the bottom up,

girder and crossbeam, rivet and plate.
For two years he grew, his height accruing
like a child's stature notched on a wall,
while up from the Narrows the body took form
from foot to hips and vaulted crotch. But where
was the rest of him, broad torso and head?
It was we who gave that image to the air,

gave it likewise to its twin across the strait
before they strung the cables, hung the roadway
amazingly into place, so that, that first time,
we drove through a space left by torn-down homes
up the approach, the Island spread before us,
the river below, and climbed into the sky.

from 20th Century Limited

This morning, I woke already pacing in my sleep
Like a man whose wife has been in labor for hours
And still the child refuses to come, turned away
Inside the womb from the cradle of waiting arms

Until he's lifted from the breach, from the wreckage
Of his mother's body that, healed again, will sail on.
So, for months I waited for the image of my father
Back from war. Then, in the half-light of a red sun

Disappearing into the Pacific, I stood like one
Of the great pitying angels in that German film I love
Who can do nothing but witness. How hard it is to pick
My father from the mass of sailors crowded at the rail

Of the destroyer easing into Navy Pier, headlands
Rearing above Point Loma and Mission Bay,
Their scrubby folds indifferent to the swell of figures
Waving banners, though there's no one to greet him.

And so, I follow where he wanders through the city,
His mother dead, his father drowned in his bottle,
Or shivering DTs in his cell on Rikers Island.
In the hours before his train departs, he hits the bars

Along the harbor, in his seabag everything he owns:
The photograph he took of a Japanese soldier
Dead on Leyte Gulf, the Luger he picked up in Oman—
Souvenirs of the journey his sons would touch and love.

Now in the luminous smoke-haze I want to rest
My hand on his shoulder like an old pal from home,
To feel his thoughts pulse up my arm like a code,
Though little comes through—there are limits to angels:

Having his hair cropped with hedge shears, diving off
The ship the way he'd dive off docks in Brooklyn,
How in the Admiralties he fished from oil-slick waves
The flesh of those torpedoed in the convoy…

His mother's face swims up, the image of his own,
The smell of apple butter in the boarding house
On Henry, running nickel beers at Kelly's Tavern.
Cat's Alley, Dollar Dye, the Gloria Theater,

Gray stones of St. Mary's Star of the Sea,
So different from this city's pristine mission walls.
The train station itself is a mission, as in the song
He used to hum about the swallows coming back.

In my father's head Goodman riffs his clarinet,
The diesel lurching east. La Mesa. Manzanita.
Names he can't pronounce, their music a piquant wind
Blown north of a border the sleeping continent ignores.

In the rocking Pullman I sit across from him, his image
In the window blending to the rewind of desert scrub
As the train fast forwards, his face morphing to the face
That surveyed the packed bar weekends at the Legion,

Stiff drinks and belly-laughs with his fellow veterans,
Him tossing me quarters for the backroom pool table.
Songs belted out to the tune of a player piano.
Wives in their bird's-nest hats and Fifties satin dresses,

Their kids fingering patterns in the shuffleboard dust,
Or outside in the scraggled hedges playing army.
Still the same crewcut, a badge of gray in the "V,"
He looks in control and vaguely discontented,

As though inside were a wound he couldn't name
But familiar to him, not like this painted emptiness,
Or the blanched distances he is unable to see—
Fired equations, the desert burned to a green glass.

Yet I'll find on his dresser that tie-clip—strange letters
Reading *NAGASAKI* buried in a jewelry case
Among his other links and pins. Is it in the seabag
Propped between his knees, the diesel swinging north

Toward the Great Divide? Having traveled so far east
He has come back west, only to press east again
Through what was once a sea of grass, sod dugouts
Of immigrants burrowed under the prairie's rim,

Their windmills whirring in the breakneck wind.
Gazing out at these cornfields, straight-edged roads
Running at right angles off the line, I can see
What my father cannot—in Red Cloud years ago

A girl sleeping with hot bricks in her bed, her eyes
A prairie sun drinking the land's iron solitude.
And now, striding along the primitive rich meadows,
Their un-ploughed innocence boundless and prodigal,

Afoot in this newer garden of creation, dense, joyous,
Modern, by all the world contributed, the burly Angel
Of these States, voluptuous, his embrace equal
To the smallest sprout, to the complete ensemble.

From the Rockies through the sandhills along the Plains
The Platte saunters toward its confluence, Missouri
And Mississippi widening slowly into the Gulf.
With little money, non-stop, my father rides this train,

Missing the juke-joints and blues bars of Kansas City,
St. Louis; missing the earthen temples—Monks Mound,
Cahokia, lost five hundred years in the American Bottom,
A farmstead cleared and raised atop the City of the Sun.

In Chicago I shadow him through Union Station,
The coin washroom where he baptizes himself home.
No time to see the skyscrapers risen from the fire,
Or catch the Dodgers on the road at Wrigley Field

Before the last leg, the 20th Century, roaring east
Through Indiana; roaring along Lake Erie's wasted shores,
Its canneries and shipyards where the homeless poet
Answered the Sirens with his true sublime.

And in my mind the line rises over Appalachian hills,
Through blunted woodland peaks to the Water Gap.
Where the train veers into its final tunnel, my father
Stares in silence at the Empire State, its sword-hilt

Gleaming over the Meadowlands, over the tenements
Where he was born, the Navy Yard, the scatter of docks
He'll work for years. And already it's flooding
Into memory, the seabag folded in the hope chest,

The watch cap buried under wedding albums, bags
Of photographs, infants' clothes, until I'm standing
Before him, no angel now, or if an angel—Rilkean,
Terrible—the hurt son staring from across a continent

Who believes these years of distance are impassible,
His face sorrowed, too, as he puts his hand on my shoulder.
And my body electric in its woundedness saying
"Do not touch me. I do not want to be touched."

Near Hag's Head

Cliffs of Moher, Ireland

This headland is the battered prow
of a ship my silent father rides
into the Atlantic. Gust after gust
buffets the raw crag of his face,
his windbreaker flapping like a sail.

He could be his own father's grandfather
the way he stands before the rail
as others stood before the hold, the blind
journey before them, and nods to me
in recognition despite the ocean between us.

Even he knows on these cliffs the dead
are reading aloud from the book of the wind.

A Cemetery in Brooklyn

Cast iron sky. A flock of gulls hovers
like scavenger angels above the city,
blocks that are beehives of teeming cells.

And in this cemetery in Brooklyn
I search with my father down side streets
of stone-encrypted names for one

that bears our own. Among baroque houses
of the dead the humbler monuments
assemble, rows of dominoes studding

the half-frozen ranges named for saints.
Through line after line of graves we circle
in our impatient dance, checking numbers

against the map's xeroxed hieroglyph
until, at the wrought iron edge of the yard,
we find the modest stone, the grave

of my father's father, William,
forgotten fifty years, never visited.
When he died at the end of the Second War

he was fifty-eight and dissipated,
his own father's age at death
(*The Tobin men never make sixty*,

I heard my aunt say once in passing),
a spoiled mother's boy sent to Rikers,
the vicious drunk who beat his wife;

though, as legend has it, brilliant,
the one indispensable engineer
at the Navy Yard, battleship blueprints

clear in his head as the special detail
tracked him to Kelly's or Kilgallon's—
Wild Bill Tobin out of Red Hook,

poor immigrant's son who married
a daughter of Southern wealth disowned
for the transgression. Ten children

and no one came to the funeral but one,
the youngest, my father, just twenty
and back from war, the scar of a dog-bite

on his upper thigh, indelible
as a father's neglect, Odysseus's wound
suffered in the flesh of Telemachus.

I see it in his seventieth year,
my father having defied his fate:
the ghost-life of his speechless hurt,

its brutal charm, the smoky bars
and car-crashes of my childhood,
how he grows more solitary every year,

rehashing stories of his close calls—
convoys shelled crossing the Pacific,
the pier explosion at Luckenbach.

Now, once more he circles the stone
before turning back to the car,
his death-wish his inheritance

and my own. I've felt it surge
under my skin, like this hard ground,
a coldness capable of anything—

though the mausoleums do their best
to seem Roman barques, or boats on a sea
where thousands tread water to keep afloat.

And someone takes it as their good work
to tend this obscure grave and others
with the patient duty of an unknown hand.

St. John

> St Mary's (Cemetery) is located at the crest of a windswept knoll,
> on the south side of Loch Lomond Road, in East Saint-John.
> There are no markers or fences to define its actual parameters…
> Mary Kilfoil McDevitt, *We Hardly Knew Ye*

On these shores
the ocean slides like a veil from the continent,
rocking tides from half a world away
withdraw
in a froth of seething dulse
where the bay's laid bare to slosh and wrack-line.
Terns print momentary braille
on the seabed shiny as shellac, and cast-up
islands appear lost Atlantises
outlasting
the incredulity of the stunned explorer,
or whale-backs for some new Brendan to mistake
before his quest resumes.
On these shores
the old city, hasped by modern bridges, stares
at itself across a river flowing
in reverse
against the Fundy as though against
itself—scale after scale of whirlpools—
and years of tourists
marveling at the gorge. Cruise ships
glide sleek hulls into the harbor,
moor at quays
along Water Street, the crowds
emptying into shops on Prince William, St. Germaine,
gentrified gargoyles
hovering like geniuses
over steam-blasted facades of the vanished wards.
On these shores
time swirls
backwards in a dream of race memory. The shipyards
brim with "shovel-fisted Irish,"
rag-heaped slovens wheeled by the remnant
of gutted townlands.

They gather
outside the waterfront's slop-bucket tenements
—Flagor's Alley, York Point—
King's Ward, Duke's Ward, Sydney Ward, Portland;
riot through the cholera-strafed streets
against Loyalist bunting and Orange drums.
On these shores
ghosts speak the lingo of lost tongues and shipwrights,
of keel and keelson,
of reamer, hauser, fid, and maul,
dead-strap, dead-eye, straker, oakum, sawpit.
On these shores
the scribers notched their signatures in timber
Brayons axed in the Mi'kmaq forests
for Cunard to fill with conifer and trade,
to return again with their starving human ballast.
The Alms House
purveyed its "fine, healthy children,
bound out
to proper persons on immediate application"—
orphan charges
discharged like slaves at auction.
On these shores
the Guatemalan restaurateur adorns his shopfront
with rainbow displays of home.
Trees canopy the Loyalist Burial Ground
in century-old growth,
while the immigrant cemetery beside the refinery
rots in its shower of acid rain.
On these shores
the *cèilidh* still thunders on late into the night
in backroom pubs
where the latest heirs
of history recede into their undreamt futures.
Lovers make love
in trashed gun emplacements,

and the new Museum rises astride the new Hilton.
But on these shores
there is no sea-road to that island off the coast
with its quarantine stations
and graveyards
where coffin ships emptied their wasted holds
—*Aeolus* and *Swan*—
the light-bearing names;
and salt winds off the Great Banks lick the Cross
raised in remembrance,
while the lighthouse signals its golden door
to an offing
that levies its apocalypse of fog over the town
from High Point to the breakwaters.
On these shores
where tombstones recede into earth like shells
below the tide,
I riffle through remains of dig books
to find my own past,
then drive with my love to the bare knoll's crest,
the stone gateposts gateless,
no walls, no boundary,
and walk among the footstones, lost avenues,
currents of grass, still ponds
of moss
fast-rising to erase the names.
On these shores
I kneel inside the empty townland of the dead
for James and the others,
travelers
who left no trace but this code in my bones,
an unmarked grave, the tern's trail
of history,
and the tide coming in with a screech of seabirds
on these shores.

The Ring

I followed the winding coast road back
from Cobh, Annie Moore and her brother
cast in bronze at the Center entrance
who were head of the line at Ellis Island,
now looking as though they inquired directions
in their own country; inside, the dim passage
through American wake and coffin ship,
the clutched figures of a prior generation
reeling to swells and sound effects, each hold
frozen in the ache of crossing; further on,
the surprise exhibit with my father's ship,
United States, steaming into the harbor
the way it steamed into the Narrows
below the rising towers of the bridge.
Above the quays, St. Colman's presided
over the dock where my mother's mother
waited for the tender, where my father's
forefather, lost in the crush, disappeared
under the raw deck of the lumber boat,
a human ballast teeming like vermin
on bodies in the fields they'd fled at home.

"I can tell you where the Tobins first landed,"
my welcoming host remarked, then invited me
to the canopied patio beside the house,
chinked glasses of whiskey neat and golden,
the garden luminous in the long twilight.
"If you drive east beyond Killeagh and Youghal
on the way to Dungarvan, off to the right
you'll come on the Ring Road, *Rinn na nGael.*
There are Tobins there still from Norman times:
St. Aubyn, Tóibín, the name gaelicized,
then anglicized into your own name now."
I had known the history but not the place.
So next day driving along the proffered route

each village seemed a station on a journey
of return. Kinsalebeg, Grange, Keily's Cross…
I had pursued the paper trail, unwound
the brede of names through census and baptism,
each generation rechristening the last,
until custom faltered like a language
on the tongue, until the trail trailed off
into the mists of the unrecorded.
Now, I was tracing a highway to origin,
the road unreeling that was once *boreen*
through townlands where the starving wandered,
their potatoes scorched black with blight
as though a fire had rained over them;
grubbers of nettles, weeds, their faces
swollen with fever, stench of *bloody flux*
rising from *scalps* where the evicted burrowed.
"Men like famished dogs scoured the fields,"
an official wrote. "I saw in one cottage
a roil of rats feasting on an infant.
Nowhere have I witnessed anything like it,
not in Calcutta, not in Dahomey—
the voiceless children silenced by hunger,
whole towns turned to habitations of ashpits,
the bodies burned at night, leaving no trace."

Descending the Drum Hills, beyond Gorteen,
I turned off the main road following signs
in a language I had lost before I was born.
This was *Gaeltacht*, remnant of the Deise,
land before the land was renamed and hushed.
What was left for me, generations gone?
A perfume of turf-smoke fresh in my nostrils:
pasture's green reach to the head and the bay;
thick fuchsia hedges; roads that were cow-paths
where locals greeted with slowly raised hands,

or a nod of the cap to my stranger's car:
the postcard my eye had framed in its longing.
Then Mooney's Pub, where I stopped for a pint
and let slip my quest. "So you're a Tobin,"
Aine said, accommodating my English.
"They're all about here. Have you heard of Nioclás,
the great singer?" She showed the photograph
with his dark hair and features, unlike my own,
though a vague resemblance to a dead uncle,
but I couldn't say for sure. What was The Ring
but another station, happened on by chance
or seeming grace? So why not trace further
through lost Norman crests, or track DNA
to nomadic tribes six thousand years gone
from the banks of the Ganges; or further back
through each human cell to African Eve,
her grunts our shibboleth tuning savannahs?

I felt the gift, shared thrumming in the bones,
later that night in the crowded room
when all the instruments had gone silent
and a man rose up shyly, regally alone,
and sang *sean-nós* one of the singer's songs:
It's a beautiful country I take you to
by the blackwater streams of the Deise,
where the thrush and the blackbird sing sweetly
and the wild deer range over the mountains,
where branches bend low with fruits and blossoms
and all the hives brim over with honey,
where the cuckoo croons the whole summer long
and the corncrake lifts its cries in the grass.

A Green Road in Clare

The Burren Way

Homesick for more than home, here, astride the sea's genius,
  I long to dissolve in a limestone landscape—
These terraced beds imprinted with grikes, the pillowed clints
  Interleaved with hollows where for eons rainwater's
Patient nibs scribed the chronicles of absence into karst,
  And still do—lines plumbing sidewise underground,
Forming a web of secret caves like halls in a dream house
  I dreamed of in my parents' house long ago.
I cannot go there, but follow the tracks' soft laneway out
  Past stile and waymarking deeper into *boireann*,
The "Place of Rocks," ocean's crushed shells and skeletons formed
  To a horizon risen from the ancient sea.
"Neither tree to hang someone, nor soil enough to bury him,"
  Cromwell lamented, having reached this graven edge,
Though had he looked, he'd have seen graves enough: tombs, raths
  Recalling playthings in a land of make believe,
Now this lost Famine village still deserted and brooding
  Where a surface river tumbles from the shale,
Its roofless walls a thriving quarter of dens and fuchsia.
  My green road itself is like a path through loss
Where Famine roads splintered, directionless, to nowhere,
  For the hungry their work a Relief without relief,
While underneath me it flows on—water's flawless love
  Honing the inner spaces, invisibly, constantly,
So along the outer faults the barren world flourishes—
  Cinquefoil, silverweed, cranesbill, gentian, orchid,
Saxifrage splitting the rocks' dappled stencils of bone.
  Rockroses burst beside the ephemeral lakes.
It's not all death, I think, this double cemetery of earth
  And thought with its sunken city off the coast,
With its "green hole" by the harbor the locals call Hell,
  And its cliffs rising from the head of the past
At the spirit's base—"Who is my father in this world?"
  Or my mother, Moher, *Mothair*, that silent "T"
My central, empty cross? What was it I meant to find

Here, now, nowhere, raging in the pitch-pipe wind:
An answer, human, out of the sublime? To be whole again?
Song mastering the wake of everything gone?
You are this longing, the iron in the wish for origin.
It sounds you, shapes you, water under stone.

My Mother's Eye

She kept it in its plastic case beside
her carousel of pills, the single contact
she wore in place of the left lens she lost
from a blown cataract. "I have to put
my eye in," she'd say, unscrewing the cap,
then would fish with her fingertip to find
that clear horizon submerged in its well,
a bubble she'd balance in the kitchen air.
She always winced inserting it, then clasped
her hands to her face as though it pained her
more than it possibly could. Before bed
it was the same, the ritual reversed,
my father stretched in his plastic-wrapped chair
watching the last of the ten o'clock news.
For twenty years I gauged her slow decline
when I'd come home, able to do nothing,
until with every visit I could trace
the lineaments of a greater distance
in the way she looked, the bride hollowed
from her glowing pose, her going under
a lone swimmer's turn away from shore.

Impossible to say what hurt her so—
something burgeoning blandly in the pool
of her diminished past, some childhood blame
for a brother's death, self-placed, or forged
out of her parents' grief, though chance whispered
the virus into his ear, into his brain.
Or maybe it was the loss of a life
she'd planned without this husband, these sons.
One late night in the kitchen's haze, her eyes
glazed over, her face wracked with drink, I saw
the unhealed glare of her long resentment:
"I always worked, two jobs when Pop got sick.
I'd just started college—all incompletes."

Her fingers squeezed a cigarette's slow burn.
"I worked nights at Woolworth's. He got sicker,
and it was pointless. Then I met your father..."
"You could still go back," I heard myself say,
"Night School." But she was shaking her head,
flesh starved to bones under her nightgown
as she poured another glass. "My life is over."
So, she thinned, the Sibyl of her own myth,
for years prophesying her imminent end.

And after it was fulfilled, I walked
through the kitchen as my father slept
alone in their bed, still stunned by her stare
that last morning when he woke beside her,
the anti-depressants she refused to take
snug in their bottles on her carousel.
A stubbed-out cigarette, her lipstick printing
its filter-less rim, lay in her ashtray.
And there, on the bright floral tablecloth,
her lens case sat, and inside—her eye
suspended in solution, floating like a cell
in the womb of its familiar waters,
unscathed, dreaming itself, waiting to grow.

The Line

Now fall quickens
to margin-less sky,

and these wild geese
arrowing the Narrows

could be Zeno's
imaginary line,

each moment's point
a fractal integer

perpetually halved
until the passage

brightens the mark
as the mark recedes

infinitely away,
the way the dead

make passage
inside, each life

with their lives
riding outward

like Máel Dúin,
Brendan, Bran

into the limitless
that seems to pause

in the Great Going,
each hastening span

a well feeding
the annals of loss,

and each life a gloss
from the scribe's nib

justified
in the needle's eye.

Outerbridge Crossing

> For me the commonplace deserves to be praised, since
> history's volcanic malice rages beneath the thin
> layer we tread so carefully…
> Czesław Miłosz, "Migrations"

As though airborne in our brief skins we follow
the rise of the ramp with other cars rivering
over the river's end of the Narrows,

the Verrazzano a huge graded bow, a crest
we ride with all the rest, everyone a world
in a cruising bubble, blood cells streaming west

through each tower's outsized needle's eye,
on either side a prospect—the vaulted city
a bed of crystals slowly accruing sky;

and out beyond the other flashing rail
Gravesend Bay churning into its offing,
each slow wake dispersing like the vapor trail

of a jet you can barely make out in the blue,
or like memory's trace when the moment passes
and it moves ahead and what moves ahead is you.

~

The flip-up seat of my parents' Rambler wagon…
The *way-back* I called it, after the time machine
on that cartoon I loved with its nearsighted dog

and boy sidekick bounding back centuries
for confabs with Plato, Shakespeare, Napoleon,
his lever's flick rectifying history.

The way-back is where I'd ride those weekends
our family would escape to the country
in that car with its monster grill and angel wings

flying over the Narrows along the new bridge,
its skyway grounded where the Ambrose lightship
guided boatloads. Gone the lightship, the ferry

that bore our numbered heads across the harbor
before it rose, emblem of the mundane sublime,
between two forts above the emptying river.

Gone now those numbered heads—father, mother—
and my own face in the way-back turning back
to find our house among the rows of huddled homes,

while ahead lay the dead-end exit beyond Todt Hill
where the freeway stopped and my father turned
for the boulevard that led past Mount Loretto

with its tapered steeple, big as the cathedral's
in that picture book I'd pore over in school,
rising over sewer-less Tottenville

and the waste-fields near the Kill Van Kull
where they'd build the new cemetery, a ridge
of the great dump visible like an alp

from this outland passage and its orphanage.
So, we drove to city's end, then over the Kill
to the final crossing. To the Outerbridge.

~

Resurrection. Outpost of the dead. No high walls,
wrought iron rails; no gothic brownstone gates
lifted like a pair of folded hands; no vaults

where the well-appointed sleep in attitudes
of their earthly glory—monuments eroding
in rain, statuary angels, that Jazz-great's

golden horn at rest on the crown of its stone.
No hills, no luminist maze of trees and glens.
Here, the storm fence measures numbered rows,

graves laid out like tract homes on flat ground
that my numbed father hardly manages to walk,
holding onto my arm as he stumbles to plywood

laid over grass and carpeted with plastic turf,
the casket propped on boards above its hole.
Mourners file behind. The priest recites his prayer

while the ritual director hands us each a rose
to lay across the lid. Rose of Longing.
Rose of Refusals. Rose of Dumbfounded Hope

that breaks in my father's hand. *Is it an omen?*
No, take mine. And then—what else to say
when saying falters?—*I'll be coming soon.*

As though in her box my mother were Penelope
each night unweaving her fate like the shroud
that crowd below will clamor to strip clean.

~

Back to Pearl Court then, the Christmas Eve
she kneeled beside the sofa unwrapping gifts
and my father laid the last box at her feet—

shock and then tears when she saw the stole
in its nest of tissue, and the whole family
ran hands along her fur-draped shoulders,

a gift never wanted because never imagined,
for the time being her lost daughter forgotten,
and everything in all our small world was now.

~

Clockwise or counterclockwise? How my father
spun the car one winter Sunday coming home
from the country, the toll plaza's tarmac

a slick rink, windows a carnival midway
of whirling lights and horns, those screaming
riders ourselves under gas jets flaming

like torches above refineries, the air
a crisp spume smoky as the atmosphere
inside the tavern we'd driven from, or

my grandmother's kitchen late afternoons
in Pearl Court, its palaver and card games,
its laughing clutches of kin and muted angers.

I wonder how he righted the car, how we ever
made it back that day across the Outerbridge,
unscathed and shaken; how we'd been furthered

by being errant, even our forgetting a motion,
slipping imprint left in the tires' wake,
our past ahead of us in the mirror's vision...

Or our future behind, what we were a summons
gnawing at the bones, until I made the journey
to fog-bound Saint John, that wasted cemetery

beside the refinery that, once, was spruce-line
declining to the Bay where terns and razorbills
still glide, freewheeling in their tangent heaven.

Below, stones crumble like sugar in poisoned air.
I moved among them, a dissimulation of one
tracing the dead's lost avenues, slabs fractured,

earth boiling up to fill the names, and me prone,
running my finger along the soluble letters
to mark the neighborhood of the unmarked grave

of James, Famine-son, my uncle's namesake, sailor
of the coffin ship that brought him here, exile
and remnant, "laborer of this city," old father

buried with others buried: Mary and Gertrude,
Arthur and Ellen, daughters and grandchildren,
all moss and scrub-grass like the rest—the dead's

immigrant townland testament to their poverty,
broken stones piled, the trees choked or dying,
those lives diminished out of lives into lives.

I thought of them as I drove back over the bridge
where the Saint John rolls into Fundy's tide-ways
and reverses itself, halted by the rocking bay

into eddies, whirlpools, a back-flowing falls,
as if the current were bent on refusing its end,
the river redoubled as if longing for its source.

~

Among the wrack of Pearl Court's decimated rooms,
buried in the afterlife of what's left behind,
I pulled it like a cache from the hope chest's tomb—

that old-time camera, its flash-arm a kind of horn
jutting from the cyclops' face, its inward eye
a shallow cave swept clean with each blink, the blank

slate of the moment at once forged and surpassed
in the shutter's click; left inside: a last reel,
along its row of portals, the horizon of the past.

I rewound it carefully as an ancient scroll.
But when it came back to me, it was as though
I looked ahead and not behind, each shot a window

where the blurred ghost-cruise sails into port,
and one where two figures stand close beside the bow,
dead mother, dead father—sunspot, penumbra.

~

Now in Resurrection their names are carved in stone
as if stone itself were not slowly lifting off
into dark energy, or whatever motion

wheels the nanosecond of each life inside its course;
for Gregory of Nyssa a forwarding and return,
apokatastasis, the soul's volta back

into the uncreated, our true home a furtherance—
flash of movement in stillness when a train
leaves its station, the hub's perfection

in the rim, each slipstream a fractal interval
of some infinite tide. And so, my mother's body
in bed beside my father spins on in its fetal

somersault; and my father's floats on his trim
of sheets, like the sleeping sailor who dreams
of home until home is the dream that stays him

from its shore; or until they are assumed
as in that photograph where they're dancing
inside the Dublin gardens the year before her death,

mugging for the camera, spurred by the name
Disco Rose to make their bodies into figures
of light the shutter limned so they could dance on.

Here, in the shadow of the Outerbridge,
I almost feel names lifting from these stones
like particles of light somewhere becoming waves;

though we'll drive back, love, over the Narrows
into our own lives, our unborn still asleep
in the womb of our choice, and Gravesend

below, lustral in its self-emptying,
as though it rode a current deeper than history,
the sky bodied in its waters, bright and ongoing.

From *SECOND THINGS* (2009)

Our mind is perplexed when we try to plumb the depth of the world beneath us. But it reels still more when we try to number the favorable chances which must conjoin at every moment if the least of living things is to survive and succeed. After the consciousness of being something other and something greater than myself—a second thing made me dizzy: namely, the supreme improbability, the tremendous unlikelihood of finding myself existing in the midst of a world that has survived and succeeded.

Teilhard de Chardin, *The Divine Milieu*

The Sea of Time and Space

> But we see only as it were the hem of their garments
> When with our vegetable eyes we view these wondrous Visions.
> William Blake, "Milton"

I.

Midsummer, and a lone bee murmurs among the lavender
along the path we've laid into our garden,
round aggregate slabs that darken in rain
under the feathery leaves of the honey locust
whose lowest branches make us bow.
We have given the body the ritual of its need,
cooked *al dente, puttanesca,* in the savory kitchen,
the tulip bowls of our glasses splashed with wine.
In after-dinner twilight still bright above the fence-line,
the compass angle of the house glows against the sky.
In such light, on Peckham Rye, Blake viewed his first vision,
the tree above him filled with angels, their wings bespangled
with stars. Thereafter, prophets appeared in the fields
beyond Dulwich and Camberwell, Lambeth Vale;
Gabriel walked with him among the shambles at Carnaby,
his spirit guide through infinite London. And, one day
God himself gazed from the casement window on Broad Street,
plain as a mother seeking her children in the crowd…
Our ancient days before this earth appeared to my mortal eyes:
inside each particle of dust the elemental strings,
behind the vegetable world the bleak Satanic mills—
gods of his own making, embodied states,
the titan walking behind the carapace of a flea.

II.

Single vision. The earth perceived merely as earth,
devoid of spirit's translucency, its light
dispersed in waves through the sea of time and space,
deranged by the gin of the unaltering eye…
One March morning, after making love, we saw

from our upstairs window a hint of green
among the brown scatter of leaves and wasted fronds
of fiddleheads, the first frail strips of crocuses,
like decorative ribbons, unblooming still,
until earth's economy compounded the scales
in hyacinth and candytuft, in phlox overbrimming
the steps, starbursts in the slow motion of its falls.
For weeks we found sprigging among the beds
pliant trunks of infant maples, their outsized
leaves spreading like river deltas, gathering light.
And we'd go uprooting, feeling in our hands the tug
of generation, its mechanism and miracle,
incessant fall of the eternal driven from sweet delight,
unless the mind revive and the body wash itself
of experience. All spring we listened to squirrels
in heat along the power lines, to the sparrows'
untraceable clamor through the trees.
You soaped aphids from the flutes of honeysuckle,
scattered shards of eggshells under the hostas
to guard them from the slugs you swore you heard
chewing each night through the darkened canopy,
their soft bellies bleeding on quicksilver trails of slime.

III.

In the suburbs of Ulro the mills whir into motion—
Case, Modine, Twin Disc, plush furnaces of Metal World.
Invisible occupants swag in the burdened clouds.
Their poisons silver the leafage after rain,
sift into soil and skin, ineradicable, resurrect
in the brute lump seething in the mother's breast.

Strange smells along the lakeshore, North Beach closed
again, beyond the Treatment Plant. Under dead stacks

at Cliffside the church-league softballers shout
for their buddy rounding third and heading home.
He has become the idea he longed himself to be
before the grind, and slides safely into reclaimed dirt.

Now, along Franklin Street—call it New Poverty Lane—
under the shadow of the genius's office tower
(his leaking monument to Nature and to Work),
the settled migrant walks beside his ramshackle home,
labors to fulfill the alderman's injunction
to beautify the town or face a fine.

This evening, in the garden, we released the last
of the ladybugs, our small effort at harmony,
their killing a necessary hunger in the balance.
And now, at the feeder, a congregation of birds
pecks at the seed. They bolt, and a jackdaw assumes
the roof, fixed eye unblinking. He caws and caws.

IV.

Today, as though all life existed to amaze us,
a dragonfly alighted on the bench where you were sitting,
gold as though daubed in golden ink, and stayed
a full five minutes, motionless as a brooch.
When Blake descended to his garden, *A Human Wonder of God*,
he'd sit naked with his wife in full view of the street,
as though their bodies had passed into translucency,
light shining through the portal of every pore.
Upstairs, the graver's tools, copper plate and burin,
took ease of their labors in the mind's illuminations:
as though, as though, until what the soul longs for
scores itself within the body's finite bounds—
creation hieratic in its web of incarnation.

Playing on their trampoline, the neighbor children shout.
Another neighbor's falcon squawks inside its cage.
Blue globes of thistle shake mildly in a breeze.
The roses, past their bloom, bleed like wax into their stems.
On his deathbed, Blake sang a favorite childhood hymn,
then disappeared, as he said he would, into "The Next Room."
Just now, as if in unison, the fireflies ascended,
emanations of the Mundane Shell, or drifting stars?
No, they are our small lanterns waking with the night.
Just now, just now, and now it is just then.
We might be under water with the bergamot and hyssop.
And the bee remains a pilgrim, aloof and prodigal,
still humming to the engines of his own bright world.

from Vessels

Mythos

In the beginning was the hand, opposable,
little god's head of a fist,

the star-shape of its mouth—toothless,
sidereal—hurling its curses

into the void. The hand wants to be
an oracle, to bestow

on the world its five-fold wisdom,
glossolalia of wants,

always the eyeless face looking
to strike. *Open, open*,

the prayer goes up. And the god
lies down in its emptiness.

Kenosis

Snake that sheds
its skin until
there is only skin
and no snake,
and the skin is this
living world.

Holy, Holy, Holy
God without
power or might.
Out of you all
things pour until
you are nothing—

a desire bedded
into the body's
lush ciphers,
sweet absence
where you touch us
now and now and now.

Goat Song

It's as though the soul
were ghostwriter
composing scenes
for the play of your life.

And you're the star,
stunned in the last act
by the blind fact
that you are who you are:

someone who's witnessed
his world renounced,
the sham announced
by roving chorus.

Oh, let Oedipus
wear the sackcloth
and gouged eyes for truth's
apotheosis—

tragedies are soaps.
Gaze clear-eyed at what
the fates serve up,
confident knowing

that even if you've
married your mother
and murdered your father
you did it for love.

Yeats at Balscadden

He labored above the impassable coast
where gulls hovered to their nests on rock,
shy youth worrying his dream-drenched songs.
He wandered below the Ben of Howth,
his self-conscious cloak flapping in a wind
that lifted the bracken's leathery fronds
in twilight descending on Ireland's Eye
and the gas-lit city he would come to hate

near sixty years on, its *paudeen* streets
a pastiche of his filthy modern tide,
hum of street lamps' pale, redundant moons
drowning the ghost-lit music of the spheres
where he stood alone on O'Connell Bridge.
Months from his own new moon, all masks
dropped, he confessed his rage at what he saw
and prayed for a third war to wipe the slate.

Forgiving himself the lot, he may be back,
a strange tourist of the new millennium
milling among the *nouveau riche*, a chorus
of cell phones perched in their hands singing
of what is to come, while the new estates
spread inexorably toward the summit.
He sees the fierce rocky faces of these cliffs
still plummeting into the stone-revising sea.

from Sketching the Galleries

Floor Scrapers

What do you make of that odd one by the door,
his silk top hat and greatcoat folded
neatly beside his chair, a sketchbook flapped
over his knees, and his eyes: flint-gray, steady—
someone staring down their own death?

To him we are the shapes our bodies make
around themselves, the *scratch, scratch* of charcoal
ferreting its trail across the blank page.
When he is finished, will he have captured
the glisten of sweat down our shirtless backs,

the taut press of our arms at the work?
I think we will be like these ringlets, stripped
layers of pigment curling into themselves,
the window behind a frame of absence,
the floor, the whole room, awash in light.

But to be as stubbornly here as this stain!
Do you see? It's not him anymore but others
crowded there, and you and I before them
whispering together, confidantes:
Soon, soon this canvas will be white again.

Sun in an Empty Room

Light that makes walls these various shades of milk
pours through this open window,
and what might be outside—you can't see it—
could be all you'd ever care to know of beauty.

If you lived here, you'd do your best
to furnish their emptiness with precious things—
luminists in which the spacious scene
appears poised to ascend, or a portrait of yourself

sketched to nervous laughter on the boardwalk.
Though why not a Fra Angelico, that courtyard
where the Virgin, a lady in waiting,
receives the angel with his brightly colored wings?

Or maybe it's a summer cottage where you wait
for family, friends, for everyone to arrive.
It might be any variety of heaven,
though it seems everything's been taken away—

these bare white walls, a floor so spare
it could be in pain. This is the house the sun lives in
like an old man who has nothing left, or a mind
brushed to transparency, the only place you wish to be.

Chin Music

Whenever I look at this photograph
that hangs beside the bookshelf in my study, I sharpen
my eyes like a batter
who trains on the curveball bending toward the plate,
trying to judge

its spin. And like a curve it seems
to defy physics, how these two once occupied the same
time and space
and still do inside this frame: The Babe as you'd expect
commanding the center,

the rest of the hunting party spreading out
the lesser of the tribe around their chief;
and there, beside him, his hair
slicked back, no longer a wild clownish ring, looking
the young rabbi:

Larry, the lowliest stooge, third fiddle
after Moe and Curly, the straight man whose antic pleas
always seemed more desperate
for having glimpsed the desperate truth. Forget Patroclus;
think instead of Achilles

in love with Caliban, or Gilgamesh
roving out for battle beside Polonius. Think of the Stooges
beside a beefcake Herakles
in a wacky Fifties riff on Homeric myth. Or, rather, think
of Everett Brundage

who owned the lodge where this photo
was taken—it had to be sometime in the Thirties—
before the Babe's moon-shot drives
arced into legend; before Larry starred with Curly and Moe
in their madcap parody

of Hilter's Germany. I have a T-shirt that reads
"I've seen the future, and it's Fine," where Larry's face
shrieks in neon
as if he'd shaken hands with a thousand volts, his whole head
flashing like an absurd Medusa.

Though when I remember Everett,
I think of a man who for years kept this lodge alive,
a taxidermist's paradise
of deer heads, antlers, bobcats, and one full-size black bear
on the fringe of big resorts.

I remember he had the keenest eyes,
that the whole raucous crowd of locals and exiles
from the city gathered
at his bar, one manifold tribe roaring on into the night.
But I remember, too,

those nights he drank until my father
closed the bar and drove him home; how he lived alone
though he had a wife
who left him; how his help—they were friends—stole quietly
from the till,

and he lost the lodge, the one thing he loved.
And whenever I remember how they found him sprawled
dead in the dive
he'd opened on the highway it makes me think of the phrase
"chin music,"

meaning a high hard one, a tough pitcher's
brush back of the batter who leans too far over the plate.
"Chin music" was what he said
that afternoon my father drove us down to the lodge
just before it closed.

On TV the pitcher reared into his wind-up,
and swooping down fired a fastball that started letter high,
and rose in a perfect
jet stream directly at the batter's head, driving him to the dirt.
"That's chin music,"

Everett said, leaning his big body
over the bar, his broad nose and wry grin not unlike the Babe's,
"it's how life plays you
before you go down for good." Do I have to say he gave me
the photo for a gift,

that I'm as awestruck now by its sheer
improbability, having watched those stilted newsreels
of the great,
the baffled mania of the stooge who took hammer blows to his head,
who had his eyes

poked out, it seemed, a thousand times?—
the Stooges, with their own chin music, that made me think
there was no pain.
In the photograph the turkey splays its feathers before the hunters,
one a hero,

one a thoughtful man who played the fool.
Did Everett take this picture, thrilled to have fame and greatness
come to this unlikely place?
The crowd fans out, mostly smiling, around the kill: Who are
all these nameless men?

Unchained Melody

One page of the newspaper splays like wings
of a seagull against the storm-fence raised
around the retreat that was a college
in the last century, before the church
renovated it, and built the old folks' home
in the same faux gothic with new cream brick.
I pick up such things, local history,
just by living long enough in one place
and never need to visit the town archives,
or the bookstore on Main, which I do,
to riffle through "the new and gently used"
and banter with the owner when I buy;
or, today, pass through empty handed
into the street, the names of buildings
still readable on the few preserved facades,
and the memory of the first occupants
more effaced than some peeling billboard
uncovered like one of Pompeii's frescos
I might read about in a newspaper—
this one, trapped against the chainlink,
a feature in the Metro section beside
Gazebo Nearly Ready for The Fourth;
though it could be headlines, election news,
a house burned in someone else's tragedy,
cars and bikes for sale, furniture and estates,
prom night previews, obits, the sports page
with its important, forgettable scores.
I'd transpose it into a blazing tree,
transfigure it to be a golden bird
or fire-fangled peacock, this urgent scrap,
scavenger flapping madly to ascend
when I happen by, lusty for symbols,
then turn the corner only to hear music
pouring—no lie—from my own house, my wife
singing madrigals—*Adieu, Sweet Amaryllis*—

and can almost feel myself beginning
to bleed like so much ink into the earth,
bleed here and now into nothing, and fly.

Of the Harmony of Celestial Revelations

O noblest greenness
who have your roots
in the sun…
Hildegard Von Bingen

I. *The Reliquary*

Here is the soul, a little golden tent
encased in stone, housing the body's dross
made holy in the foundry of the Word.

Inside its doors, the saint's flesh—tongue
and heart—flames in light beyond all seeing,
guarded by men, their hands frozen in signs,

their eyes erased by the radiance.
There is nothing now for the woman to do
but be the pure flower of her un-being,

while outside vineyards slope to the river
and a wind from the south perfumes the air
and green bells of grapes shake on their stems.

II. *The Cell*

In the beginning is vision—light a fist
to the child's forehead, the sun transplanted
into her soul as into a mirror.

In the beginning is oblation, the child
a tithe her parents offer to the abbess
inside the cathedral's torch-lit ribcage.

In the beginning is the cell—a burial,
the living tomb she vows never to leave,
at seven the child "truly dead to the world."

In the beginning are the Hours, *Opus Dei*,
the works of God sung through days like slates—
At midnight I will rise and give thanks to thee.

III. *The Sickness*

Over again that bright voice, spoken light,
the brain's dazzling scotoma perceived as God—
Ash of ash write what you see and hear,

for forty years her mind a hidden font
of secret mysteries, strange blindnesses
her eyes growing florid in their ecstasy,

the visions indisputably migrainous.
"She experienced a shower of phosphenes
in transit across the visual field."

Then I saw a woman embraced by a tree
wholly dried up, its branches enwound her,
a swarm of clouds where she lay down lamenting.

IV. *The Visions*

In vera luce. First things. The ways of God
scratched into a wax tablet on her knees,
divine gifts poured into the weaker vessel.

Here is the universe, an egg rimmed by fire,
meaning everywhere burns the love of God,
even the outermost haunts of the damned.

God's justice is a grinding stone, his zeal
against the sinner a flying head with wings.
And now appears a Man, his skin sapphire,

jewel-radiant, striding out of the light.
I see these things as in a burning mirror—
the soul and the soul's Life joined at white heat.

V. *The Language*

Blunt code. The tongue's acknowledged ignorance
scrabbled in the spirit's grammatology.
Babel and glossolalia of the soul

the saint mimics from the garbled Word.
And so this *lingua ignota*, language
invented from the speech of the Fallen

pitched to strike the heavenly registers—
Our voice is a coarse burden to the Lord—
while all around significations of leaves,

whole alphabets of stones, assume their forms,
names on a map without territory.
And the river's syntax glistens in the hush.

VI. *The World*

And what of the damned, blighted tenantry
writhing in the steel ardor of the saved?
Here is a lake like a well mouth, its stink

rising, cloud-trains of smoke on the outskirts
of heaven, Truth with its banner stretched out,
emblazoned with the heraldry of the Word.

God's justice is a pike, a burning stone,
the faithless—pigs to be cut in parts.
Above all things God requires our fear.

The saint embraces crusade and pogrom,
I am not worthy to be called a person…
And the chosen soul staggers, calling for blood.

VII. *The Glass*

So let the world be likened unto stained glass,
a rose window born of time and place,
the prism and prison of refracted light

showered from the Unimaginable.
So the light becomes the Word, the Word
the Only Begotten. So the world becomes

the image we make of it, all we have,
fallen, falsified, saved when we let it go:
the Fall is a fall out of emptiness,

the Word unknowable except by its fall,
Godhead beyond God in the small of the soul,
light within light beyond sight signified.

VIII. *The Healing*

Heat and cold. Earth, fire, water, air.
Causes in the living crux of matter
where the spirit, hidden, alchemies its cures:

for melancholy, compresses of mallow.
For sterility, convolvulus brews.
For desire, ointments of sparrowhawk.

Evil ruts in the demoniac's soul,
a wondrous worm, its sores spawning poison.
But earth is salved by the greenness of earth.

Let the afflicted sup on scraps of her bread.
Let the mad sip from the wine in her cup.
Let newborns pass through girdles of her hair.

IX. *The Greenness*

I am the fire   that keeps the fir
I am the sap   that thrills the womb
I am the murmur   in the blood

I am the ice   that seeds the rose
I am the hawk   beneath the dust
I am the flight   that stills the eye

I am the path   the body hews
I am the tree   that prunes the soul
I am the flood   that flows to God

I am the word   that speaks the flesh
I am the emerald   in the corn
I am the wind   that bears the stone

X. *The Music*

In the beginning all creatures were green,
our voices like Adam's before the Fall,
like these, antiphonal, *Eva* chanted

to *Ave* in dawn light through branching glass.
Notes like perfume, notes like budding gems,
and the world a serpent choking on pearls.

God lives hidden in a woman's body,
a Rose blooming behind the womb's shut door.
Magnificat. The dove's crystal root and salve.

The sky, all sapphire, mirrors the human face,
melisma of time and eternity.
From my wounds I stretch out my Hand to you.

Coda: The Garden

Whitest flower, creation, descendant
from Love's acetylene, and the Word itself
a purple hyacinth—these visions given

to bespeak first things, divine essences,
recede as figures of an unknown tongue
the saint chose to speak as though to angels.

Now, in the garden at day's end, the sun
pours its prodigal light through fluted bells
of columbine, dead nettle, flowering chive,

forget-me-not, a first clematis bloom.
Regard me, I would have it say, *abiding here*
among the second things bright and perishing.

From *BELATED HEAVENS* (2010)

We see the external world of stars and four elements, in which human beings and all creatures live. This neither is nor is called God. God certainly dwells in it, but the external world does not grasp Him. We also see how light shines in darkness and darkness does not grasp light, yet one dwells in the other. We also have an example of this in the four elements, which in their origin are only one element that is neither hot nor cold, dry nor wet, and yet, by its movement, it divides itself into four characteristics, into fire, air, water, and earth.

Jacob Boehme, "The Fifth Treatise On The New Birth That Is," Article 13

Westwood

Yes, you think, it's hard to be homeless
even in the interval between homes,
the one you left behind a thousand miles
where your wife remains, unweaving rooms
into boxes piled with destinations—
Bedroom, Den—and the home that waits,
you picture, like a new Ithaka, its welcome
barred by land courts, capricious gods.
Of course, you tell yourself, it won't be long,
twenty days perhaps instead of twenty years.
Still, it's hard returning nights from the job
to this house generously loaned by a friend,
under contract itself, stripped nearly bare
but for your bags and the one remaining bed
and the spindrift left of her parents' lives.

No, it's not easy to walk among remnants
of a lost world, even when it's not your own.
The antiseptic walker. The bag of shoes.
Shelves of kitsch. A jeweler's scale. Decanters.
Blunt inlays where the furniture would rest
bearing up beneath the warm familiar weight—
like casts of the rug's unalterable burden.
And on every wall an empty faded patch,
unbandaged skin, where the pictures came down.
Whatever wound you harbor with passing time
seems less and less like Odysseus's scar,
that genre piece his nurse knew from childhood,
and more and more like the raging whirlpool
he pilots toward whichever way he tacks.

Though maybe it's better not to see the journey
as some insistent metaphor that surfaces
in lives that would otherwise be their own
instead of masks for the one storied life;

better to see the name of this suburban town
as an exit sign off the interstate
from which you will move on without trial
and not an allegory of your last end,
anyone's, or gulfs stretching between stars.
Now euphony wings through the barren halls.
Pick up the phone, your beloved is calling.

Down

The many naked birds, their bodies
released after the hatching and harrowing,
praise their patience, their stunned altruism
under the knife, the carcass's largesse
of softness, each under-breast a snowfall
suspended in air, each fallen weight

of eider inside this winter comforter,
all dulcet and lace where the lovers caress—
though not as prelude to making love
for they've grown bone-tired from the long day,
and want only this modest solace
where they lie now in their proximate skins.

What did they expect the doctor to say
in the white room with its pale, diffuse light?—
the lamp a barely audible simmer, a hum,
like the echo of too many years of sun,
its silent running of photons uttered
in cloud occlusions on the body's braille.

Precautionary was the word he'd used,
and prepped each maculate interruption
along the man's back, then numbed, then carved out
what might become transfigured into flesh
that feasts on itself from the cells' hunger
as his wife waited in the outside room.

Let them rest like figures in a painting,
not the scene where the flayed god seems floating,
a feather from an angel's hapless wing,
down and down into the women's arms, but one
where dawn light christens them with dew
as if each numbered wound were gift, were grace.

Winter Storm, Jerusalem

February 2003

Not fallout, ashes, little nothing moths,
cataract spray of old wrongs remembered,
gripes, griefs, that whirling blizzard of grudges,
the gauntlet flung down like an avalanche

as the summit caves with a plosive sigh,
but this steady leveling of blown snow,
the Promised Land aswirl inside its glass dome
as though an unseen hand had shaken the sky.

Now the prayerful in their competing hats
can relinquish their faces to wall and floor,
their Gods elided out of metaphor,
their longing swept to a syntax of drifts.

All things come back; all things go on forever
the desert whispers from its dream of distance—
and this silent, white screen that falls like grace,
like manna in the marmoreal air.

Independence Day, 2005

It's not the bombs
of light that thrill, big thumps
drummed at us, time-delayed,
from our white-out war against the sky,
but it's the shapes

we marvel at,
pink and gold fritillaries, ascending
flares that burst,
silver machine-gun asterisks of hail,
rose, aquamarine.

Another explodes,
and a day-glow cube races toward us
as from some far-off
galaxy—or is it just a huge TV
flittering out?

It's Christmas,
someone shouts, when a smiley face
blooms red and green
out of the drifting fog of smoke
that looks backlit

like a movie set.
Now a glowing willow of sparks
rains for what feels
an infinite pause before the dying
cells revive,

re-animate
in what looks like whirligigs of sperm
swimming intently
for the Earth's darkened ovum
where they fall, fade.

On the river
yachts and cruise boats dawdle
under the show
safely awash in waves of flame,
while above a blimp

blazons Old Glory
in the digital clouds. Somebody
calculates each burst
amazingly for such effect
so we stay hushed

or cheer, or whoop
like the man behind us shouting *Yes*,
the mock love-cry
making some of us laugh,
in each eye

the same blinding
flashes that fury the skyline's
window mirrors,
as buildings keep standing
in a powder shower

from launch and barge.
Look: the last charges blast their tiger's face
into the night
as though we each were the tamer
it lunges for—

O I forget the name
of the mauled: was it Siegfried or Roy?
Behind us, a child
screams into the bestial teeth,
but only for joy.

The Afterlife

What's worse, nearly, than the nothing you hope it's not
Is the thought of your many dead still nearby
Watching you from behind your life's one-way mirror.

They seem as they hover behind the living screen
So close you almost sense them in the play of movement
Glazing off your own form in a shopfront window,

Like the revenants of dogged film noir private eyes
Who shadow their suspect's every move, who ghost
Their oblivious quarry by blending into the crowd.

Over time, they come to regard your every intimacy
Until you're naked as a newborn before the afterlife,
The more so since you still believe you are alone,

That your solitude, even in your happiest moments
Spent with your wife or your remaining friends,
Can be unfurled, the banner of your inmost self,

Even if it's blazoned with the pretentious seal
Of your delusion. Is it their own failures toward you
Summoning them back to the unresolving world?

Or what Agency do they report to with your foibles,
Mutterings, the wild outbursts of dread and dismay
You thought no one would hear, the unguarded rituals

Performed behind the closed doors they walk through
As if now were the moment they would make your arrest?
Though maybe they're only present like the part of you

That trails your life like a moon on a clear evening,
A new moon burning its absent reflection in a pond,
The light of its full face turned wholly to the other side.

Rogue Madonna

National Geographic Explorer

You swing through the broad high-branching trees
and what hangs from your breast, your stolen charge,
flounces like a rag doll clung to by a child
whose parents disappeared behind a train's

ashen door. You hover above, primate Eve,
as if what you hold could forever be held
past passing eons and zones occluded
by the pixilated boughs, the primeval

receding in an advent of savannah
to the long outering journey away
from your defiant primal stare, AWOL
as you are from your tribe, a savant

among your kind, who's sensed the economy
of desire, how it burgeons then withdraws—
zero bubbled to zero in the hoard.
You circuit the canopy in arabesques

clasping the dead thing to yourself, the rent
sock of your need that made the true mother
cry out, and made the others clamoring there
claw closer in common esurience.

What stuns us is not your anxious grasp,
the days of your body's failure to nurse,
so the earnest TV voice encourages,
but your pause in a kind of grim stillness

there on the limb limned by the camera's
omniscient eye, playing at the source,
the limp body fed from your barrenness.
Still, an image like some immaculate mirage

floats to mind with its flawless human face,
a radiant All-Mother gazing at us,
past us, toward some distant *Ignis*
that gathers everything into its brilliance—

we your wilier cousins, you, the living stones.
And the child on her lap also gazing out
who will die in an ecstasy of tortured
flesh, a plump icon already cognizant

of this cosmos born in waste and burials.
And you looking back, one of the going facts
beheld in your beholding as though transfixed
by the low verdant tremor of the bells.

The Executioner's Memoirs

hold fourteen notebooks,
two thousand pages,
three-hundred and ninety-five

heads, each one
expertly ex-
cised from the body's

fluent text, the steel
honed as ice,
his work charted

meticulously—
places, dates, weather,
names and crimes.

On one May morning,
Rouen, 1914,
Jacques the watch thief

was severed from
his trade. Just so
Francois the assassin,

1925, October,
who cried at the moment
the bright blade

descended, *Long live
anarchy, death
to the cops*, leaves

tumbling like coins
on the hats
of the exultant crowd.

And for forty years,
Anatole Deibler,
you were master

of your exacting
profession—*Meticulous
artisan of death,*

the auction called you,
*discreet to the point
of obsession—*

having followed
in your father's footsteps,
who had followed in his.

Pates, noggins, crania,
brain-pans, domes
of thought, each one

fell for you in the blink
of God's eye
into the basket,

until that morning
your heart
cleaved itself

while the rail hummed
like a razor along
the underground—

your eyes sharp
in the pre-dawn station,
your mind wide awake,

imagining the next
numbered head and the train
to take you to your work.

To Acedia

...like them that go down into the pit.
Psalms 28:1

Razor of nothingness, ash
Of soul thrice burned,

Thought with its armies
Of malice turned inward,

Bantam soldiers
Overrunning the field.

Slay one, a hundred
Rise to kill in its place—

A thousand cuts, and blood
An endless fog pouring

From the dustbowl
Of the heart. Languisher,

Purveyor of afflictions
In memory's back alleys,

Worm oil, searing garland,
You hawk the cold fever

That burns, liquid nitrogen,
At the raving core.

If mind were a knife
It would skin itself for you.

If skin could think,
And it does, it would

Crawl inside and sleep
For millennia,

Stupor that turns
The bluesman's song to stone.

There is only the fear
Of waking to this fuel

Consuming itself,
Consuming others—

The void's pure verb
That grows like a diamond,

A coal-black diamond,
On the tip of the tongue.

Clear Cut

From above it looks like
stubble fields, the harvest
scythed to a broad plain
of chaff, cornstalks
shucked raw, slaughtered.
But it's trees: rainforest
the size of Connecticut
gone, except the hacked
stumps, the stripped
and leveled shafts lying
as though blown down, or
slashed by a vast machine.
Who whacked them one by one?
Not us. The ant army
of the poor (who better
to blame) carts logs away,
the crumbs of extinctions
scattering behind, the rare
white tiger rarer now, while
the saw's dinosaur screech
seethes twenty-four seven.
Good thing we don't live
here, good thing we only
buy the posh armoire, paper
aggregated out of pulp,
though the sun's blades
spread across obliteration's
stunted vista, the same
as in our suburbs. Call it
Gouge Meadows. Scourge Acres.
And earth was all before them.

Dog

Black lab, runt of the litter, the one
    pet mammal allowed
in our house, and for just the week
    of her failed trial.

Manic, untrainable, irreverent,
    she came with the missiles
of October and peed everywhere,
    everywhere shat, gnawed

our mother's couch legs, pawed to tatters
    the new upholstery,
shredded curtains, slobbered the rugs,
    barked incessantly

the gruff petitions of the needy.
    In her the thinned-out
blood of the beast, shadow to Argos,
    inspired a come-back,

those nips at the hand, her trickster eye
    turned upward, as if
begging permission of the master
    to appease desire.

None of which tells why we gave ourselves
    to the playful maw,
to the raw edge of that life we kept
    at bay, then banished.

The Air Mattress

inflates out of nothing
so nothing fills
this sealed plastic sheet

elapsed on ground
while its little engine
hums in motion,

all space expanding
with the driven sound.
And under ground

the turtle of creation
swims through time,
while on his back

the world's buoyant freight
bobbles in tow
below the firmament;

or it's the god sleeping,
his oblivious cargo
a lotus risen

from his bright navel,
the universe nothing
more than his dream.

Before the dream ends
infinity wings by.
The god wakes, stretches,

then dreams the next,
that floats like this raft
with its two dreamers

under night's tent,
O pale belated heavens,
and a low wind breathes.

Giordano Bruno in Flames

Burned at the stake, February 17, 1600

A breeze's aftermath of sizzled flesh
licked the strafed cobbles of Campo de' Fiori,
bore on its serpent's back winding through brush
the last whiff of Bruno, heretical meat.

Four centuries have burned, each one a wick
consuming its essence like kerosene
since your screams—you must have screamed—erupted,
and the Roman dogs picked over your bones.

Born in the foothills of Vesuvius
with the *ouroboros* beside your crib,
you died having swallowed the universe
in your mind's feast of talismans and ciphers.

Old necromancer, numerologist,
for whom the One behind the multitude
throbbed like a wound, there is no ecstasy
like the world-lust of those who murdered you.

Figures, hieroglyphs, principalities.
The body an aggregate released at death,
launched to "innumerable living worlds."
And always at the center the Sun in stealth

dissembling in emblems, simulacra,
as though the code in each leaf were the name
of the world entire, Botticelli's *Primavera*
unlocked from the stone mortar's mash of green.

They mocked you before they lit the fire,
"Italian juggler," though you saw the atom
in the galaxy, and in their stares
your own charred finger pointing toward heaven.

But you were neither magus, nor prophet
of this boondock earth, displaced yourself: a door
through which we entered the newest orbit
between our desire and our solitude.

On this late winter morning's solstice
I walk among my yard's reluctant beds—
last fall's waste of leaves, mulch and crocuses,
the sun a white-hot rod boring through lead,

burning its blank seal into the given
that I would learn to read, had I the art.
O res ipsa, magnum miraculum.
There is no center and love is at the heart.

Lunar Eclipse

The distant band's just tuning up in the life you missed.
Michael Donaghy

Even now it darkens, vaguely occult,
a patch slipped on by a one-eyed blind man
whose haunt throbs with song, raw, Andalusian—
the kind of discordant *frission*
that pumps a healing shiver through the blood,
as if in spite of pain the Earth were good
beyond plain reason. Up there: cloud-molt
clears like cannon shot, and a hint of red
blue-shifted in the shining. Would I could
take a funicular to the aureole
to find you in the innumerable lights
with the rest of the beloved dead, the Palace
of Memory brimming and the door unshut.

A Palm Print in Lascaux

I.

I, too, want to reach behind the stone veil,
To follow the rabbit down its winding hole
Into the whisper-chamber, bosses like sails
Billowing in an earthen wind, this first world
With its presences recursive in the maze—
Bison, ibex, mammoth, and stag, the steppe
Alive in limestone on the vaulted frieze;
Down with my lamp to terra incognita,
Magician in my skin-cape conjuring beasts,
Trove of the underworld's infinite hat.

II.

Tallow smell above the axial gallery,
An island of light in the hall of bulls
Illuminates the surging cavalcade,
As if stone had fixed itself from shifting clouds
Into these forms heard by the searching hand.
Ochre hide. Black blooms of antlers splay
From a stag's head. Auroch's flaring horns.
Something in the mind cleaves to this rock face
Like a cave bear's tooth housed in its niche,
Scoured bones articulated in their graves.

III.

What hides, parietal, in the mask of dark—
After-image the child fashions in sleep,
A drunk's tremens, a screensaver's bright mark,
Virtual gallop across the humming screen?
As in a high nave curving heavenward

Where the blessed pose in their spirit ride,
So these inhuman majesties surround
The descendant. Flint-knapped, finger-fluted,
Walls move, tangible air. A horse reels, heaved
Back like a penitent: the stunned, healed soul.

IV.

The wounded man recumbent in the shaft
Awaits the bison's charge, arms outstretched
To embrace What Comes. Beside him his staff
Floats in whitewash where an all-seeing bird
Contemplates a beast, tail-up, whose horned head
Dissolves into the membrane of the vision.
Skeletal soul, mesne of the living and dead,
First émigré to the haunts of the human,
Imaginer, your shadow runs like a brede
Through the living coverts of our sojourn.

V.

Glyph-shapes, frescos, graffiti on their stall…
On Ellis Island once I saw a hand
Traced in detention beside the Great Hall,
Fingers flared like this one spit-painted
In the cave, an earth and breath communion,
As though the negative of a child's print.
When the dying tallow lamp of the sun
Burgeons to nothing and snuffs the planet
There will be just such a form to absence,
A space left in space, immaculate—

Where Late the Sweet Birds

As though I'd summoned it with the word *behold*,
A starling flew from maple leaves that hang
Above my patio, green shade, and summer cold
As fall. A plane flared overhead. Nothing sang.
Jackhammers clanged the heart out of the day
While the sun arced imperceptibly west.
The bird scavenged before it flew away,
Scraps among polynoses and the rest
Of what spring had rained down: lust's golden fire
To fill the earth with passing. It's no lie,
The wind with its sleight from *aspire* to *expire*,
And the wish I wished as the bird streaked by
Longing, in its dumb way, to make the thing strong—
The nest toward which it flew that will not last long.

Heaven

You love the conveyances of getting there—
through realms of ether by fiery chariot,
by coracle across the Western Sea,
or latched to a flying elephant's tail,
the beast descended from Indra's palace
in that Urdu story. Like Black Elk,
you might suddenly be lifted on a cloud
above wide blue plains and piled mountains
to converse at length with stallions of the air.
Or maybe, as in some strange Gnostic spell,
you'll have to recite the secret names
to rise safely above the region of Archons
who quiz the aspirant like border guards,
or bouncers at Zenith, the deity's exclusive club.
Maybe you'll travel alone, transported in dream
through porticos of light, so that everything
you've done or known or loved falls away
like shed skin, husk of self you leave behind.
Or maybe you'll ascend the scales with friends,
their names—Hopeful, Faithful, Worldly Wise—
refinements from the gray flux of your life,
so different from those earthly friends
who sustained or failed you, or whom you failed,
your denials dropped like crumbs on the path.
Or maybe, in your private *l'alta fantasia*,
Beatrice is the first crush you had at school,
Tricia Bardo, her name the perilous interval
the Buddhist dead endure to escape rebirth.
Though where she leads you—the awkward kiss,
closet games like "Seven Minutes in Heaven,"
the travails, failures, and short-lived conquests
leading to long love, sweet ease of middle age,
feels more like the journey you already made
than the one you will, the one you still fear.
How hard it is now to believe that nothing

isn't all after all, that there yet are worlds
where the dead convene in gardens or splendid homes,
naked or clothed in robes, or just in light,
and angels, their bodies unburdened of entropy,
couple for millennia with undying passion,
and where History, brutal allegory, evaporates,
so suffering finds redress, the starved are fed,
the dead reassemble in their new spiritual limbs.
At least let the last journey be like Reb Nachman's,
the celestial orchestra heard faintly at bedtime
until he wandered outside unable to turn back,
only to find himself sustained on air,
and no melodrama of souls whirling upward
in their frozen tornado of eternal praise.
Or let it be like that obscure couple
carved in relief on a cathedral wall,
among the line of souls the only two holding hands,
as though their mortal love persisted undiminished,
the Divine Life subsumed in their simple gesture,
and eternity were only a short walk together
to that still, small place where memory is healed.

As Angels in Some Brighter Dreams

For Sally, who kept the shop...

Even you gone into a world of light,
Or some metaphysical luncheonette
That smells in death of your shop's mélange—
Cheeseburger, brisket, baba ganouj.
It's seven a.m. in Eternity.
Egg on a roll, a doughnut and coffee...
The ghost-commuters queue at the counter.
You greet each with ethereal banter,
Filling every want with foreknowledge
As you did in life, poised as Queen Noor,
Magisterial behind your register.
Here at last is my Brooklyn beyond change,
Moored and palpable as any mirage.
On the wall the cedars of Lebanon
Flame green in a vale of whitewashed homes,
Your village limned by shutter and lens
Into the split second of a sixth sense.
Had I grown up in your paradise
Of biblical resplendence, an oasis—
Judging by the photograph—from the desert
Of gain and loss, hatred, self-regard,
I might have stayed, believed home the reward
I longed for, though I'd covet the promise
Of life exalted in a gleaming city.
If so, time in the village that I'd left
Wouldn't be, in the great scheme, very different
From where I found myself: the daily round
In a landscape of storefronts and row houses,
Apartment prospects with their towers
Of skyscrapers across the teeming river,
And that absence soaring above the harbor
Like a monument to anyone's lost world.
If I sit here long enough with spirits
Of the neighborhood dead eating breakfast
I might see against the iridescent haze

Of your ancient plate glass windowpanes
   My parents easing into their booth,
Regular as clockwork or ritual,
   Though they wouldn't see me, still corporeal,
On my stool-perch beside the chalk specials.
   How strange to know death made them happy.
How rich they'd seem like the others, Sally,
   Who look pleased this modest heaven is all
As they crowd in, ordering the usual.

From *THE NET* (2014)

For of Meridians, and Parallels,
Man hath weaved out a net, and this net thrown
Upon the Heavens, and now they are his own.

John Donne, "An Anatomy of the World"

The Jetty

reaches, a stone sentence, across the bay—

its jigsaw syntax entered like hopscotch
from Land's End,
                    entered the way wrens
step, step on sidewalks, crushed shells,
looking for seed,
                    as if unsure of earth,

until it feels natural to be outside
the known scope,
                    and you follow
the jumbled puzzle out farther

than you first expected, toehold
by toehold,

            to where the broader slabs
give certain footing, a way over water,

Appian, you think, miraculous
the way it seems to float
                              on tidal flats,
beach grass wavery as prairie
sprouting from wavelets, tinselate,

the whole horizon threatening to blend
earth, sky, and sea,
                though sea, sky, and earth

stand poised, pristinely, on the glinting
edge,
        so you come to feel yourself
suspended in a fluency that would be

ethereal if not for the *thump, thump*
of a festival drumming intermittently

from the town, over parabolic sands,
like finest brushstrokes lacing the shoals—

shallows of moon-snails, welks, skate-eggs,
these currents like sand coils redoubling

in pools, where shucked pilings, scarified
granite,
                    brace to colonies of rockweed
that flail in sediment's plangent ooze,

the soft siphons of lowlier lives
shooting invisibly from under,

trumpet worms, dogwinkles, bits
of swamp-pink and poverty grass

awash in foam the color of meringue,
salt-spray rust in the tide's
                                                        recursive flow,
a slow parting-of-the-waters revealing

articulations of tablets into shifting
dunes that have arranged themselves

into just this measure, as if to say
Nothing needs you here—
                                              not the sundews
and sanderlings, plovers, hovering gulls;

not even the lighthouse at Long Point,
a beacon at the brink of the human:

you are an earthstar tumbling its spores
into the living waste,
                                        the risen pleroma,

your name a net caught in the hollow
between stones
                                   while the tide sounds
the length of this transit, susurrant

fountain, a summoning from under,
and all of it gone by evening.

A Stone in Aberdaron

The poem in the rock and
The poem in the mind
Are not one.
R. S. Thomas

Driving the *Llŷn*, our tongues backed to teeth
Speaking the palette "*l*" like Bushmen,
Soft click of a key sticking in language,
We navigate coastal roads in rain

Where the Atlantic shambles to Hell's Mouth
And Whistling Sands like wind-stanched pilgrims
Sped out of the past by some fleet machine
To this shearwater church on the Sound:

Your Sound, your church—an eyrie at the crux
Of the human village and the sea,
Ancient fields weathered into bracken, brine,
The membrane of this shingle shore,

Runnels of foam in the slow tidal hush.
Obstinate priest, rock-faced, you listened
For the presence of your God like a pulse
Thrumming in the offing's ashen verge,

A whisper in the fleece of gunshot clouds.
Even now, chin deep in world, I love
Your raw vigil at the mirror's plunge,
Your rapt loneliness before the fathoms.

Here, under Hywyn's double nave, for years
You raised in faith the gleaming zero
Of the chalice rim. In the chancel's womb
You felt Christ like gritstone in the host.

For you the mind honed itself on this edge,
Your slate sublime hardened as a gem
Underground, resistant to thought, to song,
The threadbare scripts of keen equations,

Our vagrant shrines of the passing species,
And history pitiable as grass
Dunged by lost droves, while grace ran, a river
Disappearing down a swallow hole

To surface—your maker's rage, your longing—
In the depths: intimate immensity
That left you grim and brooding on the hills,
Your prayers signals beamed through shattered glass.

God was a raptor hunting you at night,
The brute vacuum portioned between stars,
Nameless well of sourceless light, sky's window,
And bone's rapture at the curtain's breath.

Your ashes scattered among these swells
Have mingled in the seething grottoes
Below bare cliffs, the seawall slicked green
As in some pre-Silurian dawn.

And there, in the scoured shallows, this stone
Big as a room, washed as if by microns
Ashore, bright-flecked, emerald, amazing.
We feel around it for the miracle

It is—rune of earth, capsule of pure time,
Lobe of the Godhead's adamantine brain.
What would you have conjured from the gift
As day's first bathers dive into the surf?

The Still Point at Craigville Beach

High above the coast and flashing ocean
where the bathers gather to stipple their feet
   with licks of surf, or take the dive,
and two boys fling their Frisbee (its motion
         something between skeet
and a hovercraft's skittering glide)

someone—it's you—leans over the
wooden porch rail of a lodge like the bow
   of that tanker churning along
the edge where sky comes down to water.
         Someone right now
could be looking back from his own sing-

ular perch, eying on shore the outline
of a bluff where they picture someone
   else scanning the horizon.
And if each of them was able to mine
         something of the other one
in themselves, perhaps the next bright wind

would carry hints of these elsewheres across
the glittering distance—the vacationer,
      arms folded like a genii
against his chest, and the one who passes,
         head cast like a coin on
the portal—you, you again, in reverie.

Meanwhile, presiding over its salt marsh,
fabulous as some outsized jungle bloom,
      the great blue heron turns
downward, inward, looking past its image
         in an undulant room.
Then wings lift, rushes—unremarked and gone.

A Starry Messenger

In the layers of one deep ravine, scientists discovered evidence
of "shocked quartz," indicative of an asteroid strike.
National Geographic, "Naked Science"

This abyssal seam
Shocked white, all matter blanching
As though at once the planet

Glimpsed the shrieking face
And its ossifying coif
Of serpents snapping

Through the atmosphere—
Six-mile flinthead, galactic
Pinball, tumbling for eons

Through the post-Big Bang gambit,
Gizmo singularity
That (if you incline

Anthropic) tips the
Euclidean dice toward us,
O provident Yucatan,

Knocking off the big critters,
Raising up the furry runts
Sleight by mutant sleight

Until we arrive,
Eve's garrulous clan, fallen
Tree-huggers, inveigling

The long grasses with our grunts,
Striding on upright haunches
Into piazzas

Where torched bonfires burn
Their living human tinder—
How quickly time's pass-

Age from opposable thumb
To disposable sums—while
The watchman stares

Into tracks of stars
Calculating amplitudes,
Surveying the hushed sublime

As in a bright gallery
Someone imagines being
The hand on the brush,

The gaze of the world
The eye makes just by looking
Remade in the practiced room—

So we know it is only
Our own strayed immensity
Caught in the signals,

Our own rogue future
Hurtling almost toward us in
The telescope's cosmic eye,

Lodestar whirled from the vacant,
Grazing air like a skipped stone
In endless ocean,

Or a contraption
In Rube Goldberg's universe,
The immense design of play

That, sometime, will wallop us
When how many billion lives
Spin in their orbits

On a day like this,
Each one with everyone gone
Gathered inside the marrow—

Yes, it could be tomorrow
When the lodestone mote bears down
And life wobbles on.

Parasitical

Despite having no lungs and unable to breathe, the second head displays signs of independent consciousness…

The first fiction is
I'm talking to you at all,
the more amorphous
of my own Janus head, the god
alive and compassing
what has gone and what
is coming, though
which is which is
hard to say. Did I say
my own? I meant ours, my
sister twin, the comelier
countenance of our mirror
linkage, orbital, locked,
each turned away one
from the other, turned
outward each to our
own horizon, inverted
reflections on the knife-
edge of a pane. Don't be
distracted by my lack
of a body, the froth
at my mouth, my eyes
circling in their sockets
like wobbling stars. I, too,
keep counsel in our shared
skull, the woven vessels
of our thoughts, the mutual
current of our separateness.
Her limbs, her length, are mine,
wayward from me outwardly,
and if you call me the one
who follows, dependent,
the monster in the blood,
think of your own, the seamless
bonds inside your boundaries

hidden familiarly; think
how each breath lives
off another's, so that in
another world, another time
we two together, one, would be
divinity in human form,
holiest, a double sun, the crown
of the temple's plenum, and I
something more than a mask
you cut free for love
of the other, who of course
will die without me; the visage
in the bottom of the tray
you'll bury to salve yourselves—
the scar, the scald, the waste,
the link, the lack: your secret face.

The Edge

Those nights my mother drank until she'd drop,
she'd rail against her husband, her sons, her life—
No bones left over in a butcher shop.

It was her gall, her private agitprop,
the protest pill against her bristling grief.
On nights my mother drank until she'd drop

the kitchen bulb burned glumly like a prop
in her personal Beckett play—comical strife?
No. Bones. Left over in the butcher shop

of her malaise, I'd swab a sullen mop
across the floor of myself and gnaw the tripe
those nights my mother drank until she'd drop

years later into the sleep that doesn't stop;
or if it does, it does where balm is rife,
no bones left. Once, inside a butcher shop,

I watched the clerk behind the counter strop
marrow into diamonds on a carving knife.
Most nights my mother drank until she'd drop.
No bones left over in a butcher shop.

Small Ode on Wave Function

The mind reels when one realizes that... all possible worlds
co-exist with us... this means that the waves of each world
vibrate at different frequencies and cannot interact anymore.
Michio Kaku, *Parallel Worlds*

On the bright other-side of the wormhole
where the lives we might have lived live on,
swirling droplets in night's entire sea,
you're like a sea creature that walked the earth,
unaccustomed stranger, until it chose
a future of fins, a memory of song.

How else should I summon you into my song
who never was, who never will be whole
or partial to the world, this world we chose?
The fin, the finger, and the face live on
in body's codes, amenable as earth
that buries and renews. Everywhere the sea

flings itself against the shore, the great sea
that widens intolerably. No song
can reach you there, though your version of earth
—too far even to say *unbeing, blackhole*—
I trust keeps and comforts: lush oblivion.
Bright faces pass us in the world we chose.

—for a daughter, not born

Greco

He'd loom in the lime-circled square of home,
His arched body shadowing the plate
That was shaped—it struck me even then—
Like the diamond sewn on Superman's cape,
And we'd watch in awe at each stung drive
He batted into orbit above the field,
Over the fence, the road, the swing, the slide;
Out, once, entirely into the lake
That looked five hundred feet from where he stood
Staring at the point receding in flight
That soared like a warp drive accruing space
Before it splashed down in our disbelief.

What fifteen-year-old could hit a ball that far?
Greco walked among us, an embodied wish
Of the life we imagined beyond our hopes—
Another Babe, Mantle, Aaron, Mays;
Not one of the crowd but one the crowd
Eyes like a sleek car behind plate glass,
Or the house you'd build in the bright image
From a glossy spread in *Fortune* or *Life.*
In the batter's box Greco tapped his cleats
As if to mime the dream he would become
And then, his ritual, his signature,
He'd bow, almost kneeling, toward the mound
To reach with his finger and touch the earth
As though he were charging some great machine
Before rising up, the boyhood myth he was—
Our sandlot Antaeus with the sweet swing,
His power summoned from the humming ground.

Not what you'd expect from a lawn man's son,
If genius can be summoned anywhere:
That modest ranch house down a gravel road
Down the road from ours, cookie-cutter homes—

Five rooms, screen porch, the walls knotty pine,
The workingman's answer for elegance.
When I'd go to dinner at Greco's house
His father spread himself at the table's head,
All three hundred pounds in his overalls.
Toothless, he stuttered. Would go house to house
Asking for work. Mowing. Trimming. Barely
Getting the words out. Unprimed syllables
Spluttering like his mower's garbled clutch.
Gap-toothed, gregarious, Greco's mother
Circled us with sausage bowls, meatballs,
A charcoal moustache tracing her lip
Nearly thick as the one her son had grown.
After the meal, Mister Greco reclined,
A sultan gouached with grass in his chair,
And would not let us rise until custom
Prevailed, and we let pass from our bodies
What he deemed a duly appreciative wind,
Lest the food we had eaten take offense
At our not announcing its place in us.

But on their living room's paneled wall
A print's lithe figure brilliant in its frame
Looked out of place but somehow aptly *there*,
Greco's El Greco, bought more for its name
Than its thrum of color, fluency of line,
Its lift-off from the human, bodies primed
Like heat waves from art's tincture and ash.
It hung across from another face of Christ,
Part rock star, part salesman hawking his heart
That flamed from the pleated drapes of his chest.
But here, crucified, the body seemed to float
Like a pale flame honed from the body's loss,
The eyes already fixed on some high beyond.
I learned years later how the man from Crete

Perfected his skill on the Byzantine,
Tempera opening windows to God,
The almond-eyed saints rapt before the Word;
Then sailed to Venice, Rome, the Renaissance
Burning in him, only to find in Spain
The mannerist refined into *mysterium*—
Clouds above Toledo, their heaving folds
Fuming above the city and its gorge,
As if stone itself had drifted into smoke.
And this transfigured man in flight from earth,
Through flesh the spirit loosening from flesh
And Heaven stooping at the brush's stroke.

Greco's father died of a heart attack,
His mother sometime after they moved
From the lake with its summer sandlot teams
Of would-be greats, our Greco, the chosen,
Who soon won notice in the wider world,
Scholarships to college and his life's wish,
An offer drafted from the major leagues—
Cut when his knee buckled blocking home,
The collision nailing him to the ground.
No comeback. No college. No Hall of Fame,
But a manager's job at a Penny's store:
Sale Days, Gift Wrap, Men's Ware, Night Shift,
Some weekends at home with the family,
His lightning body thickening at the waist.
Some seemed happy the myth had crashed,
Others looked as if to say what's left to say.
Those are the breaks, an apt reflection
For the weightless burden and the bloodless lash
That most lives come down to before they pass
Into the blind stillness of a sleeper's face—
O grace inscrutable, O monstrous grace.

A Greek Cup at the Met

In memory of Mark R.V. Southern

This crowd in smoky blackness below the rim
riotous along the tondo's reeling frieze
that looks spot-lit, as if with slip and brush
the painter fashioned revels from utter night,

could be the Yardarm's Dionysian crush
we'd join in Fridays after class, a *jorum*
or two, as the Irish say. And in Hittite,
Latin, Frisian, Hebrew, Norse, Portuguese,

Sanskrit, Saxon, Greek? You could order a pint
in any lingo, as though you'd cracked the genome
that decoded *bodhi* from *Babel*, the Beche-
de-Mer in glot's scored ogham. *We all speak Greek*,

you'd say, and showed us, tracing from English,
Yiddish, gibberish, through word-hoards in half-light,
threading back as from the plumb line of a name
to the source—your labyrinth of Ithakas

where in each the words we are make their home.
To be on parole with you, *laissez*, lazy,
once again in your *parole*—I'd make that wish
like some errant gob rubbing a phoneme bright

as a lamp: *kalyx*, its breath the aspirate shape
of this crater, its flower, its seed, the form
a root routed, ineradicable, hiding
and bound, the *gist* in the morphologist's dream.

In its wake I'd follow the vessel's curve
past parted parties and the Fates' unfolding glaze
to pull you from the whirlpool where the tide
runs darkest at the narrows and the sea churns;

pull you from the *calyx*, *Khar*, the gaping mouth;
from the *Rhibdis*, swallower, your death its design
and *Dasein*—how you'd love to find in the craw
of the beast a German cognate for *to be*.

Would what gulped you down spew you on high,
and if not here then on some other lea
where you could be the bard, us your lost crew,
where you've mastered the Esperanto of the gods.

On this meander, Mark, I see you in the brede
incised on ovened clay to the cup's empty brim,
and you're the soul the dolphin's back abides
riding wine-dark tongues of waves into the hush.

Late Bloomer

Something whispered I wanted more of myself.
That's how I turned into the *fleur* of myself.

The lake. The ripple's shimmer. That lilting face.
I'll guzzle the infinite pour of myself.

What is this flow I feel, its course through soft bone?
The current? The mother load? The ore of myself?

Fill me with all things. Empty me completely.
I winnow and still am the store of myself.

Imagine earth, the stars—all space expanding—
And finding everywhere the core of myself.

If soul's estate means a mansion's many rooms
Then someday I will take a tour of myself.

Do you think me insane, my hypocrite twin?
A catatonic's stare? The whore of myself?

Call me this. Call me that. Call me what you will.
I surpass beyond words the lore of myself.

Time blooms with space, and their sum's all I am.
I am forever the before of myself.

Beauty is Truth, Truth Beauty, Beauty is Truth…
X to nth power is the shore of myself.

Narcissus—the name a wind passing through wind.
Now watch me step through the door of myself.

Vespers Meditation at Wellfleet Bay

Moored on the glittering fabric of the waves
the boats endure each omnipresent fold
that caves on itself to become the waves
I'm watching now, improvisational waves,
meticulous ripples endlessly unwound,
it seems, from the spool of themselves. These waves
awash in their opulent world of waves
luff the hulls and bound sails stayed by knots
against the wind, though it's mild, and not
one of the gales that sometimes hurls the waves
onto the wharf that I will call my home
for now, as though I had no other home.

The wind and light that make this seascape home
magnetize distance. They also move in waves,
they also travel from some farther home
(if one can call the roiling infinite home),
not outer-ward but deeper in the folds,
the inner amplitudes of bodies—home
apportioned into Timbuktus of home.
Gazing at the bay one could feel enwound
with such similitudes, but for the wound,
an emptiness in the idea of home.
It's the thinking of it makes the knot
inside the mind, the gut, the mind the knot

unraveling—*You are what this is not,*
though this is all you'll know to be your home.
If swimming through space I saw the blue knot
of the planet floating in what it's not
I might feel like I'd been furled in waves,
myself unfurling from the fixed knot
of what I know myself to be, this knot
of particular matter. In the folds
of myself—emergent, aqueous folds—

I tack toward the offing of what I'm not
where everything that is unwinds to be wound
into new signatures that, too, will be unwound.

Knowing this seals the gravity of the wound
one feels—a black hole's all-imploding knot
would be the outward figure of this wound
if somehow the scales could be wound and wound
into a gold intricacy of home
that, by naming it, could cicatrize the wound.
Scale down. Follow to where the strings are wound,
no, wind what is, was, what will be in waves,
the melisma in which the worlds are wound.
Let light's leitmotif in-wind you in its folds.
There is only this extravagance as it unfolds.

Along the shore the sand grains wash in folds.
Micron by micron they rose, will be wound
down by forces that keep all in their fold.
I feel like Thel on the brink beyond her fold—
How is it all things are what they are not?
And clod and spirit run back to the fold
of Blake's imagined world. The beach unfolds
in broken symmetries—an expanse of home—
shattered shells, shattered stones. Away from home
families tour the wharf; invisible folds
from Wood End ruffle the air in waves.
A young girl kneels along the lulling waves.

Why do we come at dusk to worship waves
when night makes plain its penchant to enfold?
I'd know the name in which all things are wound.
I wish I knew this vastness I am not,
its everlasting flow. Light is always home.

An Echo on the Narrows

What are you, Never-to-Be, but my own voice *Voice,*
returning like light waves from outer space *space*
while the red shifting stars accelerate *accelerate*
beyond eye-shot in the all-freezing distance? *distance.*

Sometimes I think I see you through dark glass, *Glass*
plucked into being. And the dream consoles, *consoles*
of infinite strings, of far fields only *only*
separated like lives beheld at a glance. *at a glance.*

I want the world to whirl at my embrace; *Brace*
or better, you are beside a shore yourself, *yourself.*
your small hands reaching—though the winds are stiff— *Stiff*
prizing shells between the foam and currents. *currents*

And I angle my lens for light to hold *hold*
you in its sight until I am no one. *no one.*

—for a son, not born

Wittgenstein Triptych

A doubt that doubted everything would not be a doubt.
Ludwig Wittgenstein

Well, God has arrived. I met him on the 5:15 train.
John Maynard Keynes

1. *The Impossible Box*

The world is everything that is the case
Here on the page with its frozen oceans
Evolving underneath—ice, erotica,
Whole odysseys with their heaving logic
Opened. Such zones are your inheritance.
Return, and watch them kindle into ash.
Leave, and they will stifle to a mezzotint
Drained of all brilliance but nostalgia's
Insurgent stream. Ahead, tumuli
Stud horizons crepuscular with rushlight.
Even so, why not let them linger like a
Vivid inkling in the mind, a birth
Evanescing into this day or that.
Retrace the pattern back to a morning
Yawed from the straight way, zero summer sun
Telescopic, the wind your alibi.
Here is the bright center, your only Earth
Insistent in its passing, luxuriant.
Nothing fills the blue amplitude of sky
Gathering on the offing like a door.
That is where you want to be, a brochure
Homing you far from home, a leitmotiv
Assumed with the figures inside a cave
That flare on a firmament of bosses
Improvised in stone, granite cumuli.
Something in the emptiness of the world
Transmits its secret in the farthest fall—
Hollow sum seething in the quantum blur,
Elapsing *Summa*, the slow dynamo
Composed even unto the bottom-most flaw.

Alice fell through her image in glass. One,
Someone, sees past the mirror into hush.
Everything is the case. The world is that.

2. *A Cottage at Rosroe*

In the Gospels one finds huts, in St. Paul churches,
And here where Killary opens to the sea
A disused coastguard cottage where the IRA
Hid their prisoners. So, you sit shock-haired, granite-eyed
At the kitchen window chipping at propositions,
The frames and games of language like a blown gestalt—
The difficulty is to realize the groundless-
Ness of our believing—while, like every morning,
The caretaker arrives timely with milk and peat
And strews across the floor tea leaves to draw the dirt,
Then gathers the scattered drafts to burn, as if to prove
The lonely genius's trope for how you lived your life:
Philosophy is nothing but tidying up a room.
Though weren't you, too, the private at the searchlight
On the Vistula waiting for your turn at the front,
The kite maker who as a child schooled with Hitler?
And at the observation post, nightly flak and gunfire,
Nightly expecting to die—*From time to time*
I become an animal—your *Tractatus* carried
In trenches, prison camps, to the unregarding world?
Giving up your family wealth, you taught the poor;
Taught, when fame came to you, your dons-in-waiting
To turn away from academic life and work
Like a gardener whose spade uproots the wish to die,
For truth cannot be said, it can only be shown.
Which is why now you stand completely absorbed
By the shape you've traced in earth beside the path
Where you walk in the hills above the harbor,

A shape of two aspects in one, like flesh and spirit,
Before you move ahead thinking of the boat ride
You took the day before, the seabirds, the islands,
How the clouds lifted a moment from one distant ben
And sunlight rioted in silence along the rock face.

3. *The Resurrection of the Body*

You wanted it for the milkweed you crushed
In your hand, your eyes puzzling from seed
To flower, from flower to seed—*Impossible.*

You wanted it for the need, like an arm lost
In war that the soldier, a pianist, endures
Until in time he keys absence into mastery.

Didn't you say that in order to grow on
The tree must bend at a knot in the trunk
As though the tree itself were shadow of the sky,

And the spirit driven from the human
By science, by the machine, makes its return
In a mere dawn on the other side of language?

It's a picture that holds us captive, you'd say,
And like some zealous detective in pursuit
You'd grill the propositions, the clues in spate—

A clock is a bewildering instrument
Measuring a fragment of infinity,
Measuring something that does not exist—

While all your life you held at length the end
Of your passion, this stray student, that friend,
The lovers through whom you kept love crucified.

You wanted it for them, and for the suicides,
Your brothers and the countries left behind,
Ghosting you through a valley of dry bones

In which you rummaged looking for God—
Thought's virtuoso whistling Schubert, Haydn,
Consumed in a game you could not consummate:

If there is only speculation then we are in
A hell where we can do nothing but dream,
Roofed in as it were, cut off from heaven.

Though you'd have made mind as penetrating
As the doubter's finger tendered in the Savior
That could touch, touched, the manifest in the trace—

The world is *everything* that is the case.

Orpheus in *Second Life*

Their blood like mounting drums with every word
you sang, so the spurned women gathered
in their throats the shrieks that drowned
your voice that made stones and trees swoon—
then struck, then limb from limb lionized you
in the true primal way until your head,
torn from the scattered mash, floated downstream
with the singing lips, the singing lyre.
Better now that your body's been hacked to bits
to find yourself uploaded to assembling *bytes,*
to be fashioned in the image of an *avatar,*
cyber alter-ego, from *primitives, textures*
infinitely pliant as the flesh—childbirth
from olive bark, those blood drops
spawning anemones: your songs within songs.
Here, on the wide virtual continent,
in the teeming city of embodied shades,
you can live the life you might have lived
without the god's ever-pending breath
urging itself inside you. Go out among
the *matrix* of creations, morphing throngs,
faces primed like yours for a new life,
your skin alive in the digital breeze.
You are anything now you wish yourself to be—
coder, gamer, sculptor, convener of *analogs*
at embassies salient in the *metaverse*, its flawless
terms, its portals bright and bloodless.
And when *griefers* come like fickle gods
their havoc cannot harm, but only bring
the briefest lag to the lure of one's desire.
How many Eurydices await you here,
incomparably iterative in their *scripts,*
so each time together is first and last,
riskless in the mist and mass of her going.
Yes, Orpheus, better to forget the call

of your own voice, the sorrows of the rocks
and beasts, the ashen procession of leaves,
all that mourns you, and the one in shadow
whose longing out-sings your own, tempting you back
to the mauled and makeshift body of the world.

The Turnpike

...an expansion,
Like gold to airy thinness beat.
John Donne

You away, and me on the *Peter Pan*
  heading home from my own required remove,
I'm drawn by the window's broad reflection,
  the traffic passing along it like a nerve—

an endless charge of cars inside the pane:
  the voltage of the real; though as they go
sliding down its long, ethereal sheen
  where the solid world softens into flow

they take on the ghostly substance of a dream
  or, rather, what we picture dreams to be
since when we're in them they are what we seem,
  and cause us joy or pain as vividly

as the lives we think we live between the lines
  that imprint us and we pass between.
Here, the world inverts. Shades materialize
  and cars speeding left expand a breach

that transports into doubles on the right,
  and those in transit opposite condense
their mirror selves in a second teeming flight
  as if our lightship bus could break such bonds

and matter shatter. Like all things physical
  it's a conjure of parts and energies,
a Never Land of haunts inside the skull,
  though saying so won't prevent this child's cries

from jolting with their needful disturbance,
  or the aging woman across the aisle
from leaning in her slackened, palpable face—
  comically, mildly—till the infant calms.

If as scientists say we are like hurled stones,
as bounded and bound, dear, by material,
and if our minds resolve into a mist
we thinly feel to be the actual,

then who's to say the rock is not the air
it hurtles through, observed from deeper in,
not above. So you and I circuit there,
firing the inexhaustible engine.

A Rescued Copy of Radnóti's *Clouded Sky* and a Snapshot of My Parents, 1946

The blood-smear across the cover's shattered trim
Where the doomed lovers lean together the way
My parents posed in post-war photographs
Looks like a child's finger-painted swash
Of neon orange, the tantrum I might have made
Across this morning's outing in Sunset Park,
My father in what looks the murdered poet's coat,
My mother beside him, both smiling through the lens
Into the life they'll share, their years together
A winnowing to stack the heart's album of losses.

By then my own anger had grown like a root
That evening she brought it home the year I left,
A gift saved from the incinerator's miscellany
Of patient ash—*You like poetry you said?*
Is this a book you want? I found it in the trash.
Inside, the poet's terrifying angel whispered
Of saws in the plum trees and how he would end,
Lines flashing hectic on a knife's edge
Quieted by the suddenly limned face of the beloved:
You are permanent within me in this chaos.

What drew her to the bin on her way from work?
Blood's flourish? These two side by side in a scene
From her own past? Though for her husband
There'd be no forced march, no eclogues scrawled
In forest hideouts and prison camps, no mass grave
Where she would dig and find his body and his book—
The book she'd give me in this other life where love
Failed and failed and failed and still was love.
And behind each couple the bidden leaves
Blur in the gone light and wind and stay unblown.

Rambler

I got rambling, got rambling on my mind…
Afaa Michael Weaver

The jagged, red confetti
Of glass from my father's head
After he'd crashed the Rambler
Station wagon coming back
Drunk one night from a party,
My brother and I screaming
As the tree fast-forwarded
Into the crazy TV
Of the windshield while he
Dove over us at impact,
Patted like a rain shower
Starting up, drop by drop by
Drop on the grim tabletop
Of the Samaritan's house,
Bloodied gauze, and the sirens
Winding intently toward us
Like a vine of pungent sound,
The kind they call remontant,
Repeat blooms with lax canes
Bramble-like and thornier,
Freely suckering—New Dawn
Or *rosa wichurana*
That was the dashboard's color,
The same as the bouncy seats
We'd climb over to get to
The way-back where we'd look back
At the highway unreeling
Behind us as our father
Drove us onward to where-
Ever we were going: not
Malibu, not Corsica,
Places they name cars after,
Where he never went, though he'd
Buy those shiny names, wreck them,
Too, like the Fury that was

My mother's face when the cops
Brought us back, shaken, but safe—
I'll kill you, she said, in the
Doorway, *I kill you, you son*
Of a bitch, her voice caving
To the grill of the Rambler,
A chrome mouth that looked hungry
In the driveway, leering out
Of the body's glossy coat,
The body jet-black, bull-wide,
And sprouting wings like something
Out of a myth, out of a
Myth where the hero has to
Find his way back by holding
Onto a thin string, a vine
Of memory that takes him
Out of the monstrous dark, back
To the light to sit beside
A quiet pond, some petals
Floating to the shore, I said
Petals on a sky-blue pond…

From *BLOOD LABORS* (2018)

Gravesend

It is like what we imagine knowledge to be—
A firmament reflected in a sea.

The Origamist

The Cat's Eye Nebula—one could begin
there as a way of showing how being
folds in upon itself, always to form
new configurations. That's where we're from,
the vast compounded into the covert
as if all were the sum of a hidden vector;
and why I ply my art without a staple,
shaping each shear assemblage of plates
into what I wish, these bursting petals
out of a glueless flatland that I wrap
to sculpt into their own particular warp
in space and time. With me, all reduces
to a page of elementals, rescued
into some new panoply, secured
for the time being in situ—my own seducer,
enwound by the delicacy of my desire,
the artifice in which I would reside,
and do. If they remain merely these brief
renderings, they keep nonetheless the fiber
of things passing, like late afternoon pools
after showers that disappear in loops
of process, lithe, unregarded spools
that only seem intricate cuts, heart-
less, the inevitable goings of the earth.
With every misstep, with every fraught lapse,
one seeks a new ordering, sudden leaps
of the unforeseen that answer pleas,
or appear to, a twist before which failure pales.
I venture the fold, the pleat, the scar,
the code by which geometries of arcs
come clear to the mind, with every edit
harboring evidence of a new tide,
the saint behind the stain, or at the fringe
a center plain to the patient finger—
the weather's wreathe of incipient snow

in which spring's last, early layers are sown;
which is not to say in the hour of the wolf
there is no bitterness in the flow,
or the looking back brokenly at the last,
resolving then into a pillar of salt,
the fleeting prospect that was Lot's
true inheritance, his marriage to the lost.
To make these creased tessellations rife ores
out of which fish swim blindingly from roes
and all of that flaming to a rose—
is to conjure skin that skeins without a sore
as seconds famish, flourish to an era.
What I want to say, is that all we are
at core is something like an attending ear
and the world an infinitely facile veil,
the migrant medium of where we live.
Think of an expanse of winter field,
its impression that, in time, nothing's filed,
that all that was there quietly rinses
away into the whiteness, like resins
glazing in sunlight. A song of sirens
could not be more vagrant, its dis-ease
harrows and lures us as, at the seaside,
one hears a hush from the deepest shelf
that calls to every increment of flesh.
It is the lone presence of the sensual
through which the spirit sings and unseals,
like those paper butterflies a king saw
in his dream, saw they were what he was.
Hardest hatreds, scattered threads, trash, despair—
I fold, and sink, and sound, until it's praised.

Blood Labors

This cotton bud I swab under my tongue
Will crack the code of all the earth I am.
The star-crossed chancers hiding in the blood
Appear as from savannah grass, wavery
In the body's woven niche of lattices.
They walk in me as I walk in myself,
Which will end without a single passing-through—
Life hammered to the future like a wall.
Blood labors, Donne believed, *to beget spirits*,
As though its chemistry were alchemical,
Breeding what transcends from what remains.
Wind scatters dust and seeds around the scene,
From little the tallest branches breach the sky,
And that is where the birds shall make their home.

Reading Meister Eckhart at the Rock Bottom Bar

> The soul is far more closely united with God than are
> the body and soul… far closer than if one were to pour
> a drop of water into a cask of wine.
> Meister Eckhart

From the farthest back booth Kelly calls
the bar to order—tonight, Trivial Pursuits,
with Kelly ("I'm Kelly," she reminds us),
while into the emptiness inside my glass
the bartender pours another IPA
freshly tapped as from a bottomless source
ever effluent in the depths, and lifts it,
lucent chalice, cup that substantiates the froth
of my want, onto the coaster's outsized host
here in the raw thrum and rattle of time.
"Who was the first to reach the North Pole?"
Though on the page the Meister's question
posits the lure of a remoter axis:
Bullitio: the eternal boiling, primal efflux,
Godhead flowing out from Godhead into
Father, Son and Holy Spirit, a shared laugh
as the Meister tells it, of divine *jouissance*.
And where I am, as I raise my glass,
and Kelly prods with another query,
and the Keno player two seats over
scratches numbers in lead, staring at random
patterns on a screen, his dreamt riches,
appears to be a secondary flowering:
Ebullitio: this mediate stream, a current
out of eternal Confluence never-ending,
its melting forth in the shadow of nothing,
so the Meister would have it, for we are
thrown by being into multiplicity,
what we should shun, the nothing that is not,
the nothing that is, and everything virtual
as these televisions' bright, pixilated squares,
their alternate lives, the spirit rows
hierarchies doubled against a mirrored wall.

"What word makes its end its beginning?"
Kelly poses now from her niche of answers.
The mirrors here shimmer with patrons
at the rail, the greater in puzzled conclave,
and me at my book who never expected
to see Christ as a kind of palindrome,
the whole unfolding of this possible path
a flowing forward only to double back
to fare forward again, as the Meister says,
since the only purpose of God is birth—
the eternal birth of Christ in the soul,
though life in time is grief and restlessness,
and *where the creature stops, there God begins to be*,
for as the Meister knew one can't see God
as one sees a cow, and as the Meister asks
as Kelly wouldn't, "Why does the Imageless
give form to life in images when everything
must free itself from this condition,
empty itself in form and name, as the Godhead
emptied itself from itself, in the image of Christ,
Godhead beyond God an unspoken word
that utters the Word that begets the world?"
Though I see how even the strictest mind
turns to *The Daily Race*, digital thoroughbreds
captive in the illusion of forward motion,
straining along the screen for each payoff,
while *esse simpliciter*, the negation of negations,
sustains within and beyond all longing
in its Eternal Now. But now, this now,
Kelly's moved on to the obscurities
of stardom, geography, Top 40 hits,
the plots and passions of TV sit-coms—
all the drift that attaches to the mind
or does not, or floats free, unhappily,
so you fail to win the thirty-dollar gift

while that which the Meister claims you'll be
looks back on the self you have become
the way you might look at a worm in shit,
not because your life is dung and detritus
but because what it will become it is
at the core, so the Meister says, before God
was God, became God becoming, here,
where the fly and the soul lift in God's love
equally, where in Hell what burns away
is nothing, the nothing your soul embraced:
trivia, like the instruments dangled bloody
in Avignon before the old man's eyes,
Heresy is of the will, not of the intellect,
the defense of the God-intoxicated man
who had glimpsed the stillness of God's first glance
in chaff and spindrift, extravagance and stain—
God seeking Godhead in a wilderness of names.

Ode to the Google Maps Man

Gold-suited spaceman, terranaut,
Digital archon ever descending,
Eyeless, every-eyed,

You carry me with you
Down from your ether-clouded reaches
To wherever I am not,

São Paulo or Lourdes,
Seething metropolis, graffiti-blazoned
In the high, enduring sun,

The same sun pouring
On the Rue de la Grotte
Where three women in kerchiefs

Are walking, and a man
Rides his bike down the serpentine
Hillside street to the hospital.

You, too, appear
With each itinerant click
Like a vision.

That evening in the Marais,
Le Sévigné, the Place Royale,
I drank and ate and dreamed;

Or west of Clifden,
The Sky Road, the light at tipping point
To here and now and out beyond,

You transport me
There and there again, wingless, winged,
Impossible homunculus,

Cartoon bearing me back
To the forgone neighborhood
Of my childhood, the gone

Towns of former lives
Imprinting me again, blurred
Faces where cars swerve,

And these unstaged
Crossroads you station me
To browse, an array

Of storyboards, pathways
Of glimpse and glance
Tempting me to choose—

I love your wormhole
Portal that teleports
Through time, trucks, tarmac,

Florentine squares,
Odysseys of islands,
Ramshackle streets

Of Addis or Mumbai,
And you happy enough to be
Here as anywhere,

Fairbanks or Freeport,
Milan, Myanmar, Minsk,
Wellington or Wyandot;

Or floating over it all to scope
The vast empty stretches,
Waste clouds above Chengdu

Terracotta rooftops,
Tent cities, the human hives
Spreading, they look

Bacterial across
Forest and floodplain,
This writhe of a river

Idling its way to ocean,
And on His abrupt mount
Cristo Redentor,

His arms outstretched
Above the iniquitous city
Where you touch down

Again now—Icon, Voyeur,
Ever-incipient, Ever-arriving
Disincarnate,

You who hail us,
Who harry us, who haunt us
But cannot heal.

Corpse Flower, Luna Moth

The deep wine
of it risen tall above
the buried
corm,

its ornamental
spathe furrowed thought-
fully, to human
warmth.

O un-branched
inflorescence, *amorpho-*
phalos, misshapen
swelling,

with its allure
of rotting flesh
for the scarabs
to follow,

hollow, to the sun-lit
trove, as though all
dark were light
unbidden

by our parsing
eye, and love itself
hidden inside
the word.

Call it life
enrapt with death's
blight, blooming
briefly.

~

Emergent morning
in the sweetgum triggering
green, green
its wings

fanning translucent
below the porch light—angelic,
a palm of light
opening.

Hallowed, hatched
each instar inches undercover,
a spent thing
climbing

larval, alluvial,
out of every cycle's shelf-
life, its rife
unknowing,

to become this end—
brief birth flying, flown, thrown
at midnight into
beginning.

Mouthless, it appears
something bidden out of the dark,
out of the broadleaf,
unmoving,

to say something
wordlessly—the word we too
can neither speak
nor sing.

With the Gift of a Shell at H.D.'s Grave

I.

Nearly like a lyre, improvised, bone-strung
from the seething breakers, these flutings fashion
oceans falling into tide-wash—your singing
sculpted from water.
Virgo-risen, prodigal dryad, you were a
high-born hoyden *walking on the tips of grass stems*—
shore-grass, seagrass—so it was in Kensington,
wowing the salons
with your Attic goddess's measured splendor,
actress, mystic, statuesque frieze your lovers
flew to—Artemis, Hermes, Aphrodite,
living inside you.
Europe was your poet's theater, your master
barker, Ezra, fathering every longing
for the ancient purity, winter mirror,
crystalline, lucent,
that was sea rose blossoming, corm and crocus
and fracture's shining hyacinth—you always
looking startled as from a brake or a fern.
Only in marble
could you find the radiance in the shadow—
you who lived like one translated from vision,
dying as you did on a magic mountain,
lofty and homeless.

II.

Back home, in Bethlehem, your father charted
stars, but gods and latitudes gathered for you
elsewhere from this immigrant town, its mill thrum
roiling the river
winding through the Lehigh, the softened hillcrests

burdened by their past, your lost, savage country.
Had you stayed, refused the heart's choral whisper
 to be otherwise,
would you have watched the metal men descending
blackened by the furnace to forge and blow house,
iron's crystal grille crucibled to I-beams,
 skyscrapers, warships,
resined, risen out of pig iron and slag heap?
Would you have charted their passage through blastings,
molten ingots, dolomite, massive trunnions
 pivoting alloy,
finding beauty in the shale-colored bodies,
seeing in them radiant symmetries of
chiseled stone: initiates, oven-lustered,
 hammered in steel and
tempered by their Satyricon of habit;
or pass them on the street, their lives unlike yours,
privileged to have caught that high cheek turned away,
 flowering whitely?

III.

From Nisky Hill the dead regard
the river lenient in its flow,
or is it just the names that mull

each moment's flight with granite eyes
without a word? Your name complete
adorns the stone, your prone slab pressed

into the grass that flames and fails
with what you were: your crystal vein,
the kore's flare of your stricken jaw

that wooed the soirées once. Across,
the plant's Acropolis of char
broods like Mordor in its ruin,

a buttressed, fluming pantheon,
its vaulting architraves and stacks
a dead engine's monumental calm

above the traffic-hammered bridge—
iron and steel will rust away
like children's games, and all fall down.

Though here among the brethren, cast
on your abandoned ground, your grave
floats timely with the planet's roll.

And still they come as to the stone
around which the turning world revolves
leaving offerings of the sea

as at an altar—like this one,
its bloom of crossings and its shine,
its emptiness lifted like a cup.

Alchemical Meditation

It abides in secret on my pencil tip—
Greenland graphite, fossil bodies, the spans
of lost beginnings hoarded from the deeps
into softest stone across geologic time
to bring its word here for the wind to edit,
dawn quickened in folds of a stringent pool.
So life leaps from non-life, leaps outside the loop
of the un-living factum, the material pit,
to ride the sudden unfolding of a tide,
billions of years passing, before it snaps
into the billowing the sea-vents emit;
before it steadies, permeates, picks up speed
to surface dimly from the thrumming deeps.

There at the latest summit, another pool
in another random smattering of time
rounds out the new like a thought on the tip
of a tongue. To parse intent across vast spans
requires faith, or brief belief in the self-edit-
ing savvy of an always avid tide,
prodigal matter surging at Cambrian speed—
such selahs in the shales!—so another welter snaps
across scales, loop by impossible loop,
like a flicker from the Godhead's fingertip,
everything bodied, so even the stones emit
light.
        Perhaps, accounting, one might venture time
the mirror in which the Face reflecting it
sustains this aching flow from the very pit
of things, edgeless edge, below the deeps.
The longing eye looks from a shallow pool
at all that is—bridge, infinitesimal, that spans
across absence the way a synapse snaps
into mind, into place. Nothing can stem it.
Picture a loop that evolves into a loop,

how always something new leaps from the tide,
everything burgeoning borne at light speed,
though momently all looks destined for the pit.

An epitaph is not the final tip that snaps
one back into the deeps—sad, digressive pool.
The loop that is everything emits such speed
it spans the tide that will edit time, all, yes, into all.

Frond

It could be on a card, tucked away somewhere buried
In a drawer under tools, the keys to doors
Left long behind, folded like a phone number
Into the black book of forgotten friends—the name

Of that plant, tropical lenient frond we keep
By the window for light in our kitchen, each broad leaf
When young untwisting from its woody sheath
Like a scroll unfolding, patiently, out of itself

Until a mask emerges, or what looks a mask,
Triangulate, emerald, shaped like a melting heart,
Mottled in bordered squares like a turtle's shell,
Each a trim of isinglass and lustrous depth of green.

I look at the look of it and think *Les Demoiselles*
D'Avignon, each glance turned slightly otherwise
But still fixing the viewer, so when you walk away
You almost feel whatever it is beholding you

From within the painting's flourishing
Of brush and pigment, some distillation maybe
Of the model's only life, the extract the artist
Refines out of accidence. Quintessence

Would be the word, but Picasso, driven,
Used his models like demoiselles—his brutal
Need—and went through them like rented beds,
Which renders the method of transcendence

Dubious, the simile wanton. Though nights
When we turn up the Jazz and sway to Ella
Singing Cole Porter, our small tropical splendor
Nods to the softening bounce of the room

And appears to watch us giddily like the children
We'll never have, and for the moment
Everything we've done wrong feels fallen away
As I dip you, comically, not ungracefully,

To the end of the song. It's when the fluent
Leaf begins to yellow and dry, a scabrous skin,
And it dips to the counter on its weakening stem
That looks almost translucent, but elegant still

In its slim arc, that I think of your mother
On her last day, no longer able to hold her own
Head up, you holding it for her as you cradled
Her in your arms and softly patted what color

She had left back into her face that was already,
Or nearly, the mask she would wear, freshened
And pillowed, in the parlor. Yes, I think now,
There is no likeness. It just is exactly what it is—

The unrecoverable downward tilt after the names
Have been called, as one of us will call to the other
While the one leaving lifts for the last time, lifts and stares,
At what, at what one wants to ask, but does not dare.

The Creature Has a Purpose

George Keats, Louisville, KY, Christmas Eve 1841

Incongruities of the "English Palace,"
And a rush of Ohio River air,
That smells of millwork and the driven flange,
Mingle in the great poet's brother's room
Where he lies, dying of the family complaint,
The rusted bellows of his lungs giving out.
Penniless, he has become his debtors,
Having braved the Great Western Road across
The Alleghenies' broad and fordable sublime,
Their expendable grandeur mastered in flat
And keelboat, broadhorn and ark, to make
His name: two fortunes won, two sawyered
In the roiling confluence of the New World.

No death is a death of luxury—not this life
That pioneered "the Dark and Bloody Land,"
Nor the boy pent, opaque, in a Hampstead room.
Or the one who stayed and wrote and broached
His end in a far country consigned to the past,
Fountain, Forum, sun-burnished piazzas
Where posthumous lives encounter their ruin
In catacomb and column and shuttered light—
This brother absent all ends but his own.

On the mantle, the poet's portrait, wreathed
In hyacinth, Apollo's flower, looks off,
Akin to a figure on that antique vase—
All unmoving activity and scope; though
Where the poet is, now, is not the place
He sat to have this minor image drawn.
Margate is gone, and Cheapside, and Wentworth.
Which makes the brother fading here, alone,
Or tended by his slaves, a dreaming thing.
Without the social thought of thee, the poet wrote,
Nothing could stay life from *the vastness*,

The vagrant expanse of sea and sky.
And this, amid the great outpouring,
The poet against all likelihood breeching
The conditions:—*the Moon is now shining full*
And brilliant—she is the same to me in Matter,
What you are to me in Spirit—the hurt belied
On the letter's fraught, disconsolate seal:
Qui me néglige, me désole—"Who neglects
Me, torments me," the gem signaling
The poet's final letter to the beloved,
How short is the longest life. And, at the crux:
We cannot be created for this sort of suffering.

But to have stayed, or turned back, to have
Chosen sacrifice, owned that capability,
Unlike the stoat the poet glimpsed, its head
Peeping from a patch of withered grass—
The creature has a purpose and its eyes
Are bright with it? Though how to make a soul,
The poet asked, but through the medium
Of a world like this, the elemental space
That schools and scars till each becomes oneself?

He shifts a little on the bed, the one
Whose body was electric with leaving,
So he might be again at sea, sails flown
In pursuit of the Narrows, the continent
Beyond, its wonders and wealth, his offices,
Parlor life brimming with Old World ways—
The nagging neatness of a well-made life.
Under him the waters lift, purgatorial
In their predatory depths, dolphin, shark,
The greater bodies cruising, thrashing,
Scale after scale in the moon-washed swell,
A nautilus, scenting currents, scavenging,

All mother-of-pearl chambers spiraling
Logarithmic, prized, rises to the surface,
The pinhole camera of its eye open, blind
To this teeming speck of a firmament.
A breath. One more. His mouth opens,
Wider now, as if he had begun to sing.

from Downstream

Listening

How long have I been sleeping here
Naked upon this louche divan, fluid
In my sloping dream, the dream I dream
Of you in the terracotta shadows
Listening? I might be an odalisque,
Though this is no one's chamber but my own.
And yours—it is the chamber of the dream
In which I speak to you, the faintest breath
Out of Brahma's mouth, say, the fragrance
Of lotus drifting across the waters,
Or the scent of a word that comes to know
Its meaning by moving dream to dream.

River

When I rose from the river I was still
The river, and in my red hair flamed
The encircling wheels, wheels within wheels,
By which the very air around me moved.
It was then I felt my body blossom,
Orchid and trumpet flower, lily and lace,
A necklace of birds spread hand to hand
As my fingers poised to key them into song:
To be the stream and what allays the stream—
Fountain splash, dolphin leap, supernova sky.
And the nipple-hard blue mantle of my breast
Like a cold eye staring into nothing.

Islands

Now even the islands are moving,
Carried away on the ocean's current,
Stream of many streams that run downstream.
Now I see that my eyes are their eyes,
The islands' eyes, the many, searching eyes
Who look castaways from a sunken wreck—
Bird-hatted, flower-collared—that one
Whose every thought is a lily plume,
That other whose fear burns above her like gas.
If I could but be the one looking up,
The heaven-starred, of Easter Island calm,
That one island, I-land, landless: Is.

Flood

Downstream the head floats: the head of No One.
Along the floodplain and out to sea: No One.
No one sings now to the gone sky, No One.
Into the dead eyes and behind them: No One.
Each one, one thing and all things: No One.
Lullay, sing lullay, lullay sing to No One.
Echoes along the surface, into depths: No One.
Tiger blooms rise. The torn body: No One.
Orpheus dis-limbed to the bright gates: No One.
Birdsongs' adornment: this nest for No One.
Intervales of silence lift high now for No One.
No one from No one, No one into No One.

Ophelia's Garden

After the turtle shook the world from its shell,
It homed through all the waters without bounds,
Through quale and quanta, ever ascending
Until it broke the surface on the single pool
Where the dead girl floated who dove in there
And swallowed her fill until she was the pool
She willed herself in her swelled grief to be,
And so began the change, her skin turning scales,
Her breasts lifting lilies, the fronds surrounding
Inclining like mourners, while the turtle
Paddled, swimming to her palm, dandled, open,
Flowering there in the sky-blue of Krishna.

Floater

Goldfinch, grosbeak, cardinal, meadowlark
Frame me counterclockwise in my slow repose—
Eleven o'clock, eight o'clock, six o'clock, one,
Such as they've arranged themselves around
The jade leaves with their black, revolving buds.
I would compass them to the four directions.
I heard each itinerant call in my sleep,
Listened until I rose awake, feeling
The strange ferment of my eyes, their wakefulness,
And then, out of the searing, blinding coal
Of my own death flagrant on my tongue—
This violet and golden bud emerged in bloom.

Fecundity

And all shall be well, and all manner of thing
Shall grow through and out of me like a body
Made of light, my feet rooted in the Planet's
Lucent pool, its waters reflecting sky
Out of which flower fields unfold their flesh,
Such benignly eloquent wordless bouquets,
Everything efflorescence, sexy material ghost
Of me, immaculately maculate quickening
Life, bone-house birdhouse (the human hidden
In the heart's whorled foliage) and the blue
Haloes upholding twin swans curving whitely—
In me you will find no sunset, only sunrise.

Fledgling

Out of the sea's cracked membrane of stone
Struck as by Moses's staff, this island of islands,
Emergent, the tree burgeoning from deep below—
An improvised mast, an ascendant cross
Lifting its one fruit through the blue reaches,
The heavenly zones at the mind's final end:
A child's face, *imago*, heron-crowned, rising
Out of the sleeper's dream, out of the river,
Rising as anywhere forever out of blight,
Out of the boundless, out of nothing, molecule
By molecule with the perilous spin of stars—
It has been waking for a long, long time.

Early Sunday Morning on the White Pages

Not this dividing and indifferent blue.
Wallace Stevens

Whatever it is I was waiting for years ago
In that red brick apartment house where I grew up,
Whatever it is I was that ached to break loose

But had to sit cross-legged, staring out the window
Like someone staring out the window at row house yards
Identical to yards laid out in facing mirrors,

Appeared to arrive at our doorstep in the hallway
With the other volumes at the other hallway doors,
The other volumes with the same transfiguring cover

That we took inside and placed inside the cupboard
For when our book of names grew slim as our knowledge,
Or the phone number desired eluded our memory.

Though there were times I would prize it from its niche
Beside the liquor shelf and the earnest drawings
I'd crayon during weekday art classes at school

To pore over this famously deserted street
With the bright, brooding storefronts like a movie set,
Depression-era shops propped against their emptiness.

But the film must be over, the extras gone home,
And the star, stepping free of character and plot,
Walks off in his fedora from the studio's back lot

With its mock facades like these mute buildings,
The banner of an absence beheld, or the mood
A bit actor might feel in the cold water flat of his need.

The man who brushed this band of space into canvas
—Solitary windows with shades drawn or half-drawn,
Chimerical rock face, its hardness softened by light—

Knew that like light nothing permeates every brick,
That it's the dark glow of nothing behind plate glass
That was his private vacancy staring back at him,

So he could not be happy until he had defeated
The gravity in himself with scorn and silence,
And such lavish barrenness as the heart can bear.

That's why this early Sunday morning no one
Gazes out their window at the luminous dawn
Lowering the streetlamps along Seventh Avenue

As though it really were the seventh day.
That's why no one walks, dissimulation of one,
Before these barely distinguishable shop fronts,

Or stands before the hydrant and the barber pole
As if they were tribal gods of want's frozen world.
Why no one waits with an air of helpless longing

As in some bland office or midnight luncheonette
As though the puzzle of their lives had been configured
To this precisely stark arrangement of light and form.

Along the rooftops' brows a radiant bar hovers,
The ruddled facades burnish in their under-glow,
Each blunt, brilliant plane beheld into place.

Yet somehow the picture ramifies endlessly,
Still unpopulated, iterative as grass, or time neutered
Of the human in a row of wind-worn stones.

Only the viewer, like the last person on earth,
Waits an eternity for shades to rise that never will,
For lights to come on and the shadow of a face

Appear, tentatively, on the bland horizon of a sill,
For the slow, steady retinue of worshippers
To pass into then out of this street's timeless frame

The way I might have done my own Sunday morning,
Walking out the door of the building where I lived,
Like anyone hushed by night choosing to enter day,

Anyone with a name in the great book of names
Left in front of every door, every column and page
In spate behind the painting folded over like a seal

In which, like me, they might have pictured themselves
Hidden, a haunted figure waking behind the blind,
A sudden hand groping absently for the cord.

How strange the light outside illumining that scene
On your own street and the avenue descending away,
From inside the frame of your own life passing forward—

You feel its warmth. You bear the blue weight of the sky.

Of Gods and Men and Monsters

At the end of *Of Gods and Men* the monks
March side by side up a snowy mountain
Guarded by terrorists who will murder them
Off screen in the blinding grace of fog
Like a gas cloud, the stricken clutching cloth
As they do in *Gods and Monsters*—the flashback
Where James Whale, creator of *Frankenstein,*
The Bride of Frankenstein, Invisible Man, relives
The horrors endured in trench and redoubt.
The French Trappists who lived in Tibhirine,
Their monastery nearby Islamic villagers
Who came to their door for aid, give their lives
To God, willing as they do to die for love,
For Christ would never abandon his flock
And they are each Christ, like the villagers
Who happen to believe a different history.
So terror incurs the way the monster
Wakes with the wrong brain, the criminal,
And not the original the master wished.
Such is the fallen world as the monks knew,
As their Master knew, and for love of which
He died. And for love of which, this world,
Stroke-ridden, mind flickering to its credits,
Whale, "the Queen of Hollywood," begins
His last flirtation with a hunky gardener—
"Put this gas mask on," the director orders,
As the young man poses nude, the mask
Making him a Minotaur, brute animal soul
Hiding at the center of the spiritual quest…
Yes, the dying man's spurned, not unlike
His anguished creature, mute, taught to speak
By a blind hermit who too wants a friend—
Bread good, wine good—their Eucharistic meal,
Before the mob breaks in, before the bride,
Her own body fashioned from scraps,

Screams in terror with one look at her mate;
Before Whale begs his friend to kill him
Before he kills himself which he does, his body
Floating mildly in the pool's stippled sunlight,
Like light rippling the flayed air of Tibhirine…
One day he'll arrive at the door, the man
With the stylish fedora and bandaged face,
His whole body covered from head to toe
Under the fashionable overcoat and suit,
Wearing the goggles he'll remove to reveal
The missing eyes, the missing skull, before
He starts to unwind them, the bandages,
As if he was nothing but an unhealable wound.
And he is nothing, nothing, the nothing there,
Then a voice growing wilder with need,
Then the gone, gone in a rustle of bushes
Beyond the patio with the wind, as the creature
Stares from its lacework of scars—the creature
Muttering *Friend, friend* over again, the word
A puzzle, a questioning, while the hands,
Trembling, searching, the hastily sewn-on hands
Open for the offering, pleading again for love.

Arrow of Time

for Seamus Heaney

I.

After all: this world without end, Amen,
The news coming on the News, on the phone.
And it's as if I'm suddenly flung back again
To my unfledged years, your *Field Work* poems,

When something tuned in me that made me turn
Leaf by sudden leaf like a tree in wind
Until the whole tree throws itself open—
All root and writhe and airy reach at once.

By your soul's path's end, you clarified the end:
Poetry is a ratification
Of the impulse toward transcendence. Given,

And beyond *altar's dawn* and *monstrance noon.*
Still, to look inside your last look past the strand
And find the living fountain splashing down.

II.

Downpour that evening at the "Fifty-One"
Where we'd met after years, you with your word
About the book. "Enviable," you offered,
"That *gun wrapped like an infant in white cloth*"—

A boon unasked for and unexpected
From the master; and me, the fostered one,
Buoyant in that deep-trenched ratification
Still shadowed by my own *shy soul fretting.*

Our pints *throughothered* into next and next.
Talk of poems, poets—who was "the real thing"—
Till pub lights lifted and the tender shouted time.

You settled up with "the bounty of Sweden,"
Then drove me home, ever gracious, your wake
Over street-wash leaving the storm astonished.

III.

Your otherworldly grounding of that boat
From Spiritus Mundi or the Metaverse,
Its anchor altar-caught, but still afloat
In its own dimension but shored to ours

Might have shape-shifted were I the witness
To the this-worldly hull of a coffin ship,
My father's father's father's out of Cobh—
Famine ballast, steerage matter, human scrap,
Placeless in their passage from a centered place.

What caught in me was a sight of routed roots,
You keeping in touch while faring into space,
New *rungs of the air*, *signatures* for your art.

Though something else caught, too, a slippage:
The vanished, vanished, un-marveled at, un-salvaged.

IV.

Sever Hall, Harvard, Nineteen Eighty-Two,
The workshop trimmed and hunkered for the round,
Cub poems propped like bricks along a hod,

And mine, it seemed, the shakiest; or too taut
As if any wisp off the real might topple them.

You saw what was good in everything we gave
(Too generous, I thought, even back then)
But made us plumb the line, tongue-in-groove.

As for me, shanty Irish out of Brooklyn,
The blue of my father's collar still a *torc*
Around my neck, it was like I'd come upon
My name among the chosen in a storied Book
That day I spied it on your winnowed list—

And felt I might not be among the lost.

V.

I watched you walk down the aisle vested
In your tweed coat, its flecks like blood,
Clasping books to your side, your hand
Shaped more to a plough shaft than a pen,
Your poems all sphagnum and scriptorium.
From behind the rostrum your loaning voice
Quickened the still auditorium.
A tumbril of words, *Mossbawn, scree, bullaun,*
Unknown to me, deeply known,
Echoed down a long chamber inside.

So on the Narrows I would come to hear
My home as I'd never heard it before—
The seagulls screeching from Joco's Marsh,
The wind's hush lifting over Gravesend.

VI.

Yes, as it was in the beginning, is now
And ever shall be—but not, I aver,
My most honored teacher, enough reason
For holding that it's only earth bestows
Happiness or not at all; your poems
Supersaturated with the afterlives
Of scapulars, stations, *In Hoc Signo,*
The dead with their particular blood,
And Christ's lines in the dirt your metaphor
For making poems. Only one *steeped in luck*
Could judge this life fit for keeping going.

That said, may you lift off as in life
From ground into air into Bright Nowhere,
The heart's parted curtain holding open.

Bulk

According to some recent physicists, our four-dimensional space constitutes a "brane" that is merely a part of a higher dimensional reality called "the bulk."

Far off in the unsayable distances
Beyond effect and cause, our own vast
Membrane no bigger than a nanochip
In the still vaster assemblages, the bulk
Hunkers, endless stack, infinite sum,
Barnacle lashed to the whale of itself
Cruising to no home, nowhere near here
Where on the far side of the stockade fence
Between facing yards our neighbor ventures
Outside her house, a screen door slamming shut,
Then smoker's cough on the guttering porch
Glimpsed between weathered gray slats,
Or wondered at through a passing veil of leaves
From the deck above: her hoard, her detritus.
How long since we'd heard her husband died?
For years on weekends his music blared.
Saddened for her, but not alone in being
Glad for the quiet, we worried our respects
Across the gulf of our differing lives,
And kept that quiet when her daughter's shouts
Echoed outside the peeling clapboards
To please stop, she was pleading, her drinking.
Years since, the quiet has settled in,
Her presence signaled by her clotted hacks,
Insistent, massing. She moves among them,
The unused tables, haphazard chairs,
Scattered playthings on grassless ground,
The dog-less doghouse, and at the lot's edge,
Wedged in by growth, monumental, moored
To nothing but its own floored gravity,
A delivery truck, mottled gray, rust-worn,
No sign of what goods it once had carried,
Windows fogged with grit, the ancient wheel still,

As if, somehow, it has always been here,
Always will be, while the satellite lens
Pulls back, panoptical, into its ken
With the blown weight of every receding thing.

La Cicada Família

Like an old Victrola, its needle stuck
  In the groove where the flamenco dancer
Patters her firecracker feet to the floor,
  Machine-gun maracas, so the cicada
Pays homage to its clattery muse,
  She who pitied the flight of Tithonus
Withering eternally through his dog days
  As the myth tells us, unable to die,
His timbals buckling to fashion song,
  The shucked body transfigured
With its losses, a wanton, wending
  "Come hither" to the beloved—
Wings like a window's beveled glass,
  The female slitting a twig's bark
To lay its eggs so the nymphs, newborn,
  Can drop, shimmering pink shower,
To the ground to feed on plant roots
  For the five instars before emerging,
Magicicada, after seventeen years
  Into imago, to sing its risen song again,
Dithering hum, dizzying ascension,
  Like a mass exodus of souls from the earth.
And what lifts the heart is another longing,
  Sagrada, to picture Gaudí laboring
On the nave that would become his crypt,
  The temple accruing niche by niche
In slow time like a holy mountain—
  God's body in rock, a radiant *parlante.*
The nudity of the beggar is seen
  Through his rags, he would say, whose eyes
Friends remarked were piercing blue seas.
  Though he would engineer the spirit
From the opulence of trash, crockery,
  Bedsprings, broken tiles and toys—
All found their place in habitations

Of the fabulous, improvisations, geometry,
Montserrat's high womb, Tarragona's light,
Oven linings, needles, metal bands, shards.
Nature, he felt, abhors the monochrome.
So he daubed his surfaces with *objets trouvés*,
Cameos and collage, unbuttressed ascent,
Grotto, diorama, carnival and shrine,
Desiring to capture in his flares and folds
The plastic reality of the spiritual world.
And so behold the metamorphosis
Of turtle into forest into catenary sky,
Snail and sunflower, a quickening of leaves,
All things in *trencadís*, parabolic flight,
The soul's promise in a liturgy of stone.
In his last months he slept among them,
The uncompleted forms, the dreamt facades,
And kept like clockwork his daily ritual,
Morning Mass, angelus, late confession, prayer,
While in between he hammered out
His plans, a universe rising alluvial
(God, my patron, is in no real hurry)
On the luminous *troposfera* of the Baix Camp.
So he walked the restive streets of the Ramblas
Honing his vision, to heal through material
The nightmare of materialism, working
Like a minimalist of the monumental scale,
Seeking the equilibrium of earth
And heaven—*cicada, sagrada—La Sagrada*
Família, with its numbers and symbols
Of creation's mosaic, its four facades
For Nativity, Passion, Judgment, Resurrection,
Its eighteen steeples spiraling inwardly
Like a nautilus, with its transept cross
Marking the infinite directions, with its excess
And absence like the Mystical Body.

When the tram struck him that June day
  Ten years before the Civil War (the anarchists
Would ransack his grave, burn his plans),
  No one recognized the great man bleeding
On the ground, pants secured with safety pins,
  His shoulders swimming in his suit,
A handful of nuts and raisins in his pocket.
  So they carried off the coppersmith's son
Who would ride his donkey through Ruidon,
  A sickly boy, troublesome birth, and died
Like the homeless, broken among the poor
  Whom he loved, master of play and praise,
Genius whose art was a frozen music.
  So on his final day in his unfinished *templum*
He closed his prints, a hush like a plainchant
  Of folding wings, calling to his assistant,
My friend we must come back early tomorrow
  So together we can make more beautiful things.

That Is to Say

Dr. Nathan A. Scott, Jr.

Fall, and the terraced ascensions of this Lawn
Buzz with the callow treasons of its clerks,
        And along the colonnade
The sun makes a gnomon of each column and brick
Where light waves congregate astride their opposite
        On every wire-edge of shade.

From above, the Rotunda's unblinking eye
Looks up, looks back as though from where it came,
        Some archetype or figure,
And not a built thing imagined into presence
By faulty, human genius on the backs of slaves—
        A wound that would nurse its cure.

From higher still, let's say a satellite map,
With every turning threshold of range and scope
        The center grows center-less,
An assemblage of "dreamy anonymity,"
Strangely depthless, a flat and fracturing collage
        Of small lives moving en masse

Like passing circuits across a motherboard
No matter their ambitions or pains, no matter
        But matter animated
By what you called the frailest "fragments of adjustment"
Our idea of the world a frontier in extremis,
        Derelict, desolate,

Which is to say, as you would say, what you saw
As a fall and a forgetting, a banal eclipse
        That leaves us in the meantime,
An erased horizon, and earth unchained from its sun.
What good, then, apropos of nothing, to savor
        The fine meal, the martini,

The chatty communion of friends at home,
The calling of others to learn otherwise?
        I only want you to see,
The great saint wrote, which was the creed you lived by
And what you taught, a way of making poetry
        A way of letting-be,

Until the part could somehow cicatrize the whole,
The cheap synecdoche like an empty sequined glove
        Become a bright beholding.
As in Bearden's *Return of the Prodigal Son*
Where the one who's come back looks stanched in gauze,
        Humbled, raw, his enfolding

Waiting in the advent of those who greet him,
Themselves radiantly particulate
        With scraps, bits—surfaces
The artist improvised on this kaleidoscopic frame
Where the one who's escaped the sty's stench and mire
        Turns outward from the faces

Of those who will embrace him, of those he will embrace,
Toward us as toward a lens, his chest shining
        With its breastplate of shook foil,
The cast-off bottle that bound him secured in rope,
His two horizons behind, the ashen and the risen,
        And that candle at the fulcrum

Under the figure's wide, iconic eye, burning
As in a tabernacle—so you would have us see
        Each such meeting together
As a ritual of color, depth of field, the promise
Of an imminent All-in-All that flashes instantly
        In every instant's shutter.

That is to say, as you would say, everything
Is threshold, and is so by way of being
        Providently on the way,
Itself and not another thing, and so the advent
Of a coming home: it is the slug's slim prayer
        That teaches how to pray,

Riding its losses across a patch of ground,
Till one believes with each leaving in the kinship
        Of things that do not look akin,
The circle squared in a turn of the scope. That is to say,
We are gathered wherever we go by way of love,
        And nothing will be forsaken.

Coda

Swallowtail, Variation

Turning
from my book, I find
this next life

newly freed of its
ornament hanging
from the sheerest

veil of fennel,
obsidian wings like
hands in prayer,

bright vestures
of yellow-green, a slick
wash on wood

where the novice
flesh must have
tumbled, already

the dear predators
circling
with their honed

fascination.
What to do
but lift it from

its vessel,
like a host in my palm,
to let it go?

NOTES

Dusk, Empire: New Poems

Epigraph from the theologian and philosopher Augustine of Hippo (354-430), Sermon 80.8 in *Essential Sermons.*

"The White Road": Caminante, no hay camino:"Traveler, there is no road," by the Spanish poet, Antonio Machado (1875-1939).

"Fable of the Alternative Fact" is for Alan Soldofsky.

"Triumphs and Laments": after the South African multi-media artist William Kentridge.

"Gleninagh": In Irish "the valley of ivy," a townland in Northwest Clare. "An fear gorta," the hungry man or the hungry grass, a phantom that represents the Great Famine.

"The Lesson": John Keats is "the young poet" and the italicized words are from his poem "Bright Star."

"Swallowtail": for the murdered child, Bella Bond (2012-2015). Her body was discovered in a garbage bag on Deer Island in Boston Harbor. Italicized text is from Augustine of Hippo.

"The Ruin": My translation of the Anglo-Saxon poem from *The Book of Exeter.* The final lines of the poem have been lost, so I have filled them in using loss as a reflexive metaphor.

"The Sand Painting": with gratitude to Jericho Brown for inventing the duplex form. The penultimate line of the poem alludes to Isaiah 42:1.

Where the World is Made

"René Rilke": Rainer Maria Rilke (1875-1926).

"Boethius in Downstate": Anicius Boethius (480-524), Roman philosopher, author of *The Consolation of Philosophy* written in prison, put to death by Gothic Emperor Theodoric under suspicion of treason. Downstate is a medical center in Brooklyn, renowned for its psychiatric care.

"Stylite": is for William B. Thompson.

"If You Cut Your Finger, Bandage the Knife": after the German artist Joseph Beuys (1921-1986).

Double Life

"Homage to Bosch": after the Dutch painter Hieronymus Bosch (1450-1516).

"Human": See Dante, *Purgatorio*, Canto XXIII, lines 31-33.

"Miranda": See William Shakespeare's "The Tempest."
"Homage to Bartolomé de las Casas": The Spanish clergyman, writer, lawyer and activist Bartolomé de las Casas (1484-1566). Juan Ginés Sepúlveda (1490-1573), the Spanish humanist and philosopher.

The Narrows

"The Narrows": *causey*, Irish usage for causeway; *clachan*, a haphazardly arranged cluster of farmhouses in Irish townlands; *cottier*, a laborer bound to a small parcel of land; *déori*, Irish for "exile"; *meitheal*, system of cooperative seasonal farming common in pre-Famine Ireland; *rundale*, pre-Famine system of land distribution in which smaller and smaller parcels of land were made of use to ever larger numbers of Irish peasants; *throughother*, a permission of passage through adjacent fields; *Tír na nÓg*, The Land of Eternal Youth in Irish lore, associated with America.
"Pallbearers at Emily Dickinson's Funeral": *immram*, literally, "voyage" in Irish journey lore, as in *The Voyage of St. Brendan* or *Máel Dúin*.
"A Mosque in Brooklyn": The poet is W. H. Auden in his poem "Archeology." The last image of the poem alludes to Farid ud-Din Attar's *The Conference of the Birds*.
"At the Tree of Many, One": The title, like the form of this poem, alludes to William Wordsworth's "Ode: Intimations of Immortality." The ancient hymn is the Gnostic "Hymn of the Pearl."
"20th Century Limited": The epigraph is from Homer's *The Odyssey*, Book 16.
"St. John": The poem's form alludes to Louis MacNiece's "The Hebrides." The island referred to is Partridge Island in Saint John, New Brunswick, a quarantine station during the influx of Famine Irish.
"The Ring": The last lines of this poem are my free translation from the Irish "Cois Abha Móire na nDéise," "The Blackwater of the Déise," sung by the late Nioclás Tóibín (1928-1994) of Rinn na nGael. The Déise names the territory in the southeast of Ireland that later became Waterford and parts of surrounding counties after the British conquest and the colonial re-naming of the land.
"A Green Road in Clare" and "The Line" appeared in *The Net*, but complete the book-length sequence of *The Narrows*. "The Line" should be read as the first poem in section XI before "The Rainbow Café," and "A Green Road in Clare" should be read as

the last poem of the same section after "Afterlives" in the book, *The Narrows.*

"Outerbridge Crossing": St. Gregory of Nyssa (335-395 CE). In his theology *apokatastasis*, universal salvation, is the return of all things to God, even, eventually, the damned.

Second Things

"The Sea of Time and Space": Details from William Blake's life were derived from Peter Ackroyd's biography of the poet.

From "Vessels": The Greek word *mythos* means "plot" or "story" and forms the root of the word "myth." The Greek word *kenosis* means "self-emptying." In Philippians 2:5-11 the word is used to describe the emptying of God's divinity into the humanity of Jesus.

"Yeats at Balscadden": In his teens, William Butler Yeats lived briefly at Balscadden House on Howth, a peninsula on the Irish Sea north of Dublin. "Paudeen" is Irish slang, commonly used as a derogatory or dismissive reference to Irish countryfolk.

"Of the Harmony of Celestial Revelations": Many of the details of the life of St. Hildegard von Bingen (1098-1179) are in Sabina Flanagan's *Hildegard of Bingen: A Visionary Life*. Perhaps the greatest of the Rhineland mystics, Hildegard was a poet, painter, musician, composer, naturalist, healer, and theologian. Some of the poem's images derive from her work *Scivias (Know the Ways of God). In vera luce*: Latin for"in the light of truth." *Lingua Ignota*: Latin for "unknown language." The phrase refers to a language invented by Hildegard to bring human speech closer to that of the angels. The title derives from her symphony for voices.

Belated Heavens

"Westwood" is for Martha Rhodes.

"To Acedia": Better known as sloth, acedia is one of the seven deadly sins, closer in spiritual effect to clinical depression than to laziness. The epigraph is from Psalm 28.

"Giordano Bruno in Flames": Giordano Bruno (1548-1600), Italian philosopher, cosmologist, alchemist, priest, and early proponent of the idea of an infinite, non-hierarchical universe, as well as the idea of God's immanence subsuming the multiplicity of all things. *Res ipsa, magnum miraculum* translates as "the thing itself, the

great miracle."
"Lunar Eclipse": in memory of Michael Donaghy (1954-2004).
"Heaven": The last line alludes to Czesław Miłosz's epigrammatic "Memory and memory" in his "Notes" from *Bells in Winter*.
"Where Late the Sweet Birds": This poem plays bouts-rimés with Shakespeare's Sonnet 73.
"As Angels in Some Brighter Dreams": The title alludes to Henry Vaughan's "They Are All Gone into the World of Light."

The Net
"A Stone in Aberdaron": for the Welsh poet R. S. Thomas (1913-2000).
"A Greek Cup at the Met": in memoriam, the linguist Mark R.V. Southern (1961-2006).
"Wittgenstein Triptych": for the Austro-British philosopher Ludwig Wittgenstein (1889-1951).
"Orpheus in *Second Life*": In the multiplayer on-line game *Second Life*, a virtual world, one designs avatars out of "primitives," templates of script that are elaborated into any form desired. "Griefers" are participants who cause others trouble. In Ovid, Orpheus reunited with Eurydice in the Elysian Fields after the Maenads dismembered him.
"On a Rescued Copy of Radnóti's *Clouded Sky* and a Snapshot of My Parents, 1946": The Hungarian Jewish poet, Miklos Radnót (b. 1909), was killed on a forced march by Nazis in 1944. A notebook containing the poems for his posthumous book was discovered in his coat pocket after his body was exhumed from a mass grave.
"The Turnpike": the epigraph is from John Donne's "A Valediction: Forbidding Mourning."
"Rambler" is for Afaa Michael Weaver. The epigraph is from his poem "Rambling."

Blood Labors
"Gravesend": this cento's lines are from Elizabeth Bishop's "At the Fishhouses" and John Keats's "Endymion."
"Blood Labors": the italicized phrases are from John Donne's "The Ecstasy."
"Reading Meister Eckhart at the Rock Bottom Bar": Meister Eckhart (1260-1328), one of the greatest mystical theologians of the Christian West, faced charges of heresy in 1326. He died before the Papal See decided his case.

“With the Gift of a Shell at H.D.’s Grave” is for Hilda Doolittle and Bob and Stephanie Watts.

“The Creature Has a Purpose”: details owe much to Denise Gigante’s *The Keats Brothers: The Life of John and George.*

“Downstream” consists of twelve voice retablos after twelve paintings by Eleanor Spiess-Ferris.

“Early Sunday Morning on the White Pages”: for the American painter Edward Hopper (1882–1967).

“Of Gods and Men and Monsters”: inspired by the English film director James Whale (1889-1957).

“Arrow of Time”: in memory of the Irish poet and Nobel laureate Seamus Heaney (1939-2013).

“La Cicada Família”: for the Catalan architect and designer Antoni Gaudí (1852-1926).

“That is To Say”: the American scholar and theologian Dr. Nathan A. Scott, Jr. (1925-2006) was the author of more than twenty books, and held two distinguished chairs at the University of Virginia.

Acknowledgments

I am deeply grateful to the sustaining support of Martha Rhodes, Ryan Murphy and everyone at Four Way Books for seven of my previous collections, as well as to Middlebury College Press and Louisiana State University Press. Special thanks also to the editors of the following publications where the new poems in *Dusk, Empire* first appeared: *Alabama Literary Review, Berfrois* (England), *Classical Quarterly, The Common, The Common Online, The Hudson Review, Literary Matters, Measure, The Other Journal, Plume, Queen Mob's Teahouse* (England), *Salamander, Zócalo Public Square, Plume 9* (Canisy Press, 2021), and *Open-Eyed, Full-Throated* (Galway: Arlen House, 2019). I am also grateful to Christine Casson, James Fraser, Joan Houlihan, James Rogers, Aidan Rooney, William Wenthe, and Ryan Wilson for their judicious contributions about which of my poems to include, to Aidan Rooney and William Wenthe for helpful suggestions on new work, and to Jonathan Blunk for his exceptional editorial attention to these poems.

About the Author

Daniel Tobin is the author of ten books of poems, most recently *Blood Labors* (2018), which the *New York Times* and *Washington Independent Review of Books* named one of the Best Poetry Books of the year, and *The Mansions* (2023), a trilogy of book-length poems which won the Human Relations Indie Book Award and the National Indie Excellence Award in Poetry. A suite of versions from the German of Paul Celan, *The Stone in the Air*, was published in 2018, and a chapbook, *Gloss Arias I: From the Distances of Sleep*, appeared in 2025. He is the author of several critical studies, among them *On Serious Earth: On Poetry and Transcendence* (2019) and *The Odeon: Essays on Poetry* (2025), as well as the editor of *The Book of Irish American Poetry from the Eighteenth Century to the Present* (2007), and *To the Many: Collected Early Works of Lola Ridge* (2018), which received a Special Commendation from the Poetry Society (UK). His many awards include the Massachusetts Book Award in Poetry, the Julia Ward Howe Prize, the Stephen J. Meringoff Award, and fellowships from the National Endowment for the Arts and the John Simon Guggenheim Memorial Foundation.

Four Way Books is grateful to those individuals who participated in our Build a Book Program. They are:

Anonymous (10), Robert Abrams, Debra Allbery, Maggie Anderson, Kathy Aponick, Sally Ball, Jean Ball, Victor Basta, Adria Bernardi, Richard Blanchard, Laurel Blossom, adam b. bohannon, Lee Briccetti, Anthony Cappo, Anne Babson Carter, Cyrus Cassells, Jennifer Christman, Peter Coyote, Kwame Dawes, Michael Anna de Armas, Brian Komei Dempster, Patrick Donnelly, Lynn Emanuel, Joan Frank, Rigoberto González, Rachel Eliza Griffiths, Catherine Grossman, Naomi Guttman and Jonathan Mead, Beth Harrison, Jeffrey Harrison, KT Herr, Carlie Hoffman, Melissa Hotchkiss, Thomas and Autumn Howard, Parker Howe Foundation, Catherine Hoyser, Linda Susan Jackson, Elizabeth Jackson, Liz Janik, Marilyn Johnson, Deborah and Maria Jonas-Walsh, Elizabeth J. Kandall, Maeve Kinkead, Lindsay and John Landes, David Lee and Jamila Trindle, Rodney Terich Leonard, Howard Levy, Owen Lewis and Susan Ennis, Ralph and Mary Ann Lowen, Maja Lukic, Ricardo Alberto Maldonado, Donna Masini, Cleopatra Mathis, Lupe Mendez, Dale Neal, Mary Jane Nealon, Kathy Nelson, Marilyn Nelson, Nicole Nevadunsky, Kimberly Nunes, Rebecca and Daniel Okrent, Cathy McArthur Palermo, Marcia Pelletiere, Megan Pinto, Martha Rhodes, Paula Rhodes, Laurie Rosenblatt, Lyris Schonholz, Soraya Shalforoosh, Jennifer Skeele, Mary Slechta, Page Hill Starzinger, Sarah Stone, Yerra Sugarman, Marjorie and Lew Tesser, Reed Turchi, Maria Walsh, Martha Webster and Robert Fuentes, Calvin Wei, George Whalen Jr., Mark Wunderlich, Kathleen Zimmerman, and Carol Zoref.